MICROWAVE BASICS

DELICIOUS, EASY RECIPES FOR YOUR MICROWAVE

Pat Jester

CONTENTS

ANOTHER BEST-SELLING VOLUME FROM HPBooks®
Publisher: Rick Bailey; Editorial Director: Elaine R. Woodard
Editor: Jeanette P. Egan; Art Director: Don Burton
Book Assembly: Leslie Sinclair
Typography: Cindy Coatsworth, Michelle Carter
Director of Manufacturing: Anthony B. Narducci

Published by HPBooks, Inc.
P.O. Box 5367, Tucson, AZ 85703   602/888-2150
ISBN 0-89586-396-0
Library of Congress Catalog Card Number 85-81327
© 1986 HPBooks, Inc. Printed in the U.S.A.
1st Printing

Material from Microwave Cookbook
© 1982, 1983 HPBooks, Inc.

Cover Photo: Chicken Quiche, page 48

Introduction

GETTING TO KNOW YOUR MICROWAVE OVEN

This guide will help you enjoy the full potential of the most revolutionary addition to today's kitchen—the microwave. Revised standard recipes and delicious new ones demonstrate the time-saving versatility of this exciting appliance.

In-depth information and full-color how-to photographs will enable you to make the microwave work for you as never before. You will find many useful tips for adapting your favorite recipes so they can be cooked in the microwave.

This incredible appliance is geared to your busy lifestyle. Get to know it with the help of this book. The following questions and answers give information that is basic to cooking a wide range of foods in your microwave.

Q. What are the main advantages of cooking with a microwave?

A. Compared with conventional cooking, the greatest advantage is fast cooking time for all but a few items. This in turn saves energy and reduces the heat output into your kitchen, a tremendous plus during the summer. The fast cooking encourages maximum retention of vitamins and flavor in vegetables and other foods.

Q. Can you stir or check food in the microwave while the oven is operating?

A. The microwave power will automatically shut off when you open the oven door. Check on the food, close the oven door and then restart the microwave. Or, if the food is done, turn the timer to OFF.

Q. Can you change power levels while the microwave is operating?

A. You certainly can. If food is boiling too hard, for example, change the power to a lower level to cook more slowly. It's similar to using a burner on top of the range.

Q. What are microwave hot spots?

A. Most microwaves have one area that has a concentration of microwaves and consequently cooks food more quickly. This explains why it is necessary to stir and rearrange foods or turn dishes during cooking. This action rotates the food through the hot spot and contributes to even cooking. Some rearranging is also recommended for ovens with the carousel or rotating feature.

Q. How do you know where the hot spot is in a particular microwave?

A. Watch which area of food in a large casserole starts to bubble first or which area of cheese on top of a casserole melts first. This is a good indication of where the hot spot is.

Q. Why does the amount of food affect the microwave cooking time?

A. Unlike conventional cooking, 6 baking potatoes will not cook in the same length of time in the microwave as 2 potatoes. Foods have to absorb microwave energy in order to cook. More food absorbing microwave energy means less microwave energy is available for each item. The same is true for the contents of a casserole. The amount in a large casserole takes longer to heat than the amount in a small casserole.

Q. What other factors affect microwave cooking times?

A. The starting temperature of food affects the cooking time. Frozen peas, for example, take longer to cook than canned peas that start at room temperature. The shape of food also affects microwave cooking times. Microwave ovens cook food from the outside toward the inside. Therefore, thin foods cook faster than thick foods. The center of a dish heats more slowly than the edges. Select foods that are uniform in size and shape for more even microwave cooking. The composition of foods also affects the microwave cooking time. Foods high in fat and sugar cook faster in the microwave.

Q. Which utensils can be used in the microwave?

A. Refer to your manufacturer's use-and-care guide. Generally, ovenproof glass, ceramic and pottery dishes, including clay pots, with no metallic trim or parts, oven cooking bags and frozen-food pouches can all be used for microwave cooking. Paper should be used only for short cooking times. Plastics vary widely; check the plastic cookware package description to find plastic utensils recommended for microwave cooking. Some will melt or distort, especially if used with foods high in fat or sugar content. Baskets and wooden boards without any metal parts can be used in the microwave for brief reheating of foods such as rolls. Many specially designed microwave utensils are available. They include browning skillets, plastic or ceramic meat-roasting racks, fluted tube dishes, muffin dishes and ring molds.

Q. Which utensils cannot be used in the microwave?

A. Metal in any form should not be used unless the manufacturer of your oven states otherwise. This includes metal twist ties and dishes with decorative metal trim. There are two reasons for this. The most important is that it may cause *arcing* which looks and sounds like lightning or sparks inside the oven. The other reason for not using metal is that it reflects microwaves away from itself rather than allowing them to pass through the material and cause the food to become hot. This shielding effect of metal can be used to advantage when cooking large items such as roast meat or poultry. During the longer cooking time required for these items, some areas tend to cook faster than others. To prevent overbrowning, these areas can be shielded with small pieces of foil held in place with wooden picks. Never allow the foil to touch the oven walls.

Q. How do you know if a dish is safe to use in a microwave?

A. Place 1 cup of cool water in the microwave beside the dish you are testing. Microwave at 100% (HIGH) for 1 minute. If the dish is warm, it is absorbing microwave energy and should not be used in the microwave.

Q. Is it true that food cooked in the microwave comes out looking pale?

A. Baked goods and meats that are cooked in a very short time do not have the browned appearance we are used to. If you feel that this is a disadvantage, here are some ways to overcome it. You will find recipes in this book for glazes to make the appearance of poultry and meat chops more attractive. The browning skillet called for in some recipes is particularly recommended for cooking steak. You can also use one of the color-enhancing products now on the market. Frosting or a number of toppings using ingredients such as brown sugar, spices and nuts can be added to baked goods to increase their eye-appeal.

Tips for Microwave Cooking

Give dish a half turn—If the skillet is given a half turn, the tomato in the bottom skillet will be in the same position as the tomato in the top skillet.

Give dish a quarter turn—If the dish is given a quarter turn, the pear in the bottom dish will be in the same position as the pear in the top dish.

Pierce or prick—Pierce foods with membranes or tight skins, such as egg yolks, oysters, chicken livers and baked potatoes.

Ring molds—Ovenproof glass, plastic and ceramic rings are available. Or, place a glass or ceramic baking cup in center of a pie plate.

Browning skillets—A special substance on the outside bottom of these skillets causes this area to become extremely hot.

Shielding—Use small pieces of foil secured with wooden picks to cover areas that are over-browning or becoming warm during defrosting.

Deep casseroles and baking dishes—Both utensils hold 2 quarts. Be sure to use a deep casserole when it is called for in a recipe.

Cover—Use a casserole lid unless the recipe states to cover in some other manner. Or, cover with vented plastic wrap, opposite page.

Cover with paper towel—Use white paper towels to cover foods that might spatter and require only a loose cover.

Cut a small slit in pouch—The red "X" marks a 1-inch slit that should be cut with a knife to vent frozen pouches.

Cover with waxed paper—Use waxed paper for a loose-fitting cover that allows steam to escape.

Stir—Always stir outside edges toward center and center toward outside edge. The outside edges will cook first.

Cover with vented plastic wrap—Either fold back a corner as on the squash rings or cut a few small slits with a knife.

Rearrange—Move items from the center to the outside edge, and items at the edge to the center.

Appetizers & Beverages

Lengthy cooking time is eliminated with the microwave. Keep a few basic ingredients on hand and you will be able to serve speedy snacks when friends drop in.

Q. What are the advantages of cooking appetizers and beverages in the microwave?

A. Many appetizers, such as cocktail meatballs and stuffed vegetables, are precooked but require reheating before serving. The microwave does this quickly and efficiently. Individual servings of beverages can be heated or reheated in mugs using the microwave.

Q. What appetizers and beverages do not cook satisfactorily in the microwave?

A. It is extremely dangerous to attempt any kind of deep-frying in the microwave. This means that deep-fried appetizers, such as egg rolls, cannot be cooked in the microwave. Breaded snacks and puff-pastry appetizers will not cook well. Drinks with a high proportion of eggs, such as eggnog, can only be warmed or they will curdle.

Q. How are appetizers and beverages cooked in the microwave?

A. Dips with cream-cheese bases are heated at 70% (MEDIUM HIGH) until they begin to get warm. Cracker toppers with cream-cheese or mayonnaise bases are warmed at 30% (MEDIUM LOW). Cocktail meatballs and franks heat quickly at 100% (HIGH), as do sandwiches, stuffed mushrooms and stuffed artichokes. Stuffed oysters heat more gently at 50% (MEDIUM). It's easy to toast nuts, seeds and coconut in small batches at 100% (HIGH). Snack mixes in large volumes toast slowly at 30% (MEDIUM LOW). Most beverages are heated quickly at 100% (HIGH). Some are brought to boiling at 100% (HIGH) and then simmered at 30% (MEDIUM LOW) to develop flavors.

Q. How do you know when appetizers and beverages are done?

A. Drinks and soups without eggs are heated to 170F (75C). Be sure to stir drinks and soups to distribute the heat before deciding whether they are ready to serve. Dips with a cream-cheese base should be just warm; they may curdle if they become hot. Sandwiches should also be heated until just warm or the bread will be tough and dry.

Q. How do you convert favorite beverage recipes to the microwave?

A. Most drinks without eggs can be easily adapted if you compare them to a similar recipe in the chapter.

Q. Are any special utensils needed for preparing appetizers and beverages in the microwave?

A. A large heatproof pitcher, 1- and 2-quart glass measuring cups and heatproof mugs are all useful for microwaving and serving hot drinks and soups. You can use trays made of wood or straw and straw baskets for warming food in the microwave. None of the utensils should have metal parts.

Cooking Appetizers

Many precooked appetizers, such as cocktail meatballs and stuffed vegetables, are ideal for reheating in the microwave.

Do not attempt to deep-fry any kind of food, such as deep-fried zucchini. Dips made with cream cheese should only be heated until warm to prevent curdling.

The microwave is perfect for cooking individual servings of soups and beverages. Stir to distribute the heat. Soups and beverages without eggs should be heated to 170F (75C).

Top to bottom: Savory Cheese-Stuffed Mushrooms, page 10; Bacon-Nut-Stuffed Artichokes, page 11; Spinach-Stuffed Appetizer Oysters, page 11

Curried-Chicken Snack Sandwiches

1 cup finely diced cooked chicken
1/2 cup finely chopped apple
1/4 cup raisins
2 tablespoons chopped celery
2 tablespoons chopped green onion
2 tablespoons chopped peanuts
2 tablespoons mayonnaise or salad dressing
2 tablespoons plain yogurt
1 teaspoon curry powder
5 or 6 (4-inch diameter) pita-bread rounds, halved
    crosswise, or 12 to 14 party-rye-bread or Melba-toast
    slices

To garnish:
Apple slices

1. In a medium bowl, combine chicken, apple, raisins, celery, green onion and peanuts.
2. In a small bowl, mix together mayonnaise or salad dressing, yogurt and curry powder. Combine chicken mixture and mayonnaise mixture; toss lightly to mix well.
3. Spoon filling into pita-bread halves or spread on party rye bread or Melba toast. Place in a circle on a round 12-inch microwave platter. Microwave at 100% (HIGH) 2-1/2 to 3 minutes or until filling is heated through; give platter a half turn after 1-1/2 minutes. Garnish with apple slices. Makes 5 to 6 servings.

Traditional Hot Cocoa

1/4 cup unsweetened cocoa powder
1/4 cup sugar
1/4 cup hot water
3-1/2 cups milk
1/2 teaspoon vanilla extract
3 or 4 large marshmallows

1. In a deep 1-1/2-quart casserole with lid, thoroughly blend cocoa powder and sugar. Whisk in hot water until blended. Cover and microwave at 100% (HIGH) 2 minutes.
2. Gradually whisk in milk. Cover. Microwave at 100% (HIGH) 7-1/2 to 8-1/2 minutes or until heated through; whisk every 2 minutes. Whisk in vanilla.
3. Ladle cocoa into 3 or 4 mugs. Top each serving with a marshmallow. Arrange mugs in a circle in microwave oven. Microwave at 100% (HIGH) 1-1/2 to 2 minutes or until marshmallows are puffed. Makes 3 to 4 servings.

Savory Cheese-Stuffed Mushrooms

1/2 cup herb-seasoned stuffing mix
1/2 cup shredded Swiss cheese (2 oz.)
1/4 cup chopped parsley
1/4 cup finely chopped water chestnuts
2 tablespoons chopped pimento
3 tablespoons water
1/2 teaspoon chicken-bouillon granules
12 fresh mushrooms, 1-1/2 inches in diameter
2 tablespoons butter or margarine

To garnish:
Pimento strips

1. In a medium bowl, combine stuffing mix, cheese, parsley, water chestnuts and pimento; set aside.
2. In a 1-cup glass measuring cup, combine water and bouillon granules. Microwave at 100% (HIGH) 30 seconds or until water boils and granules have dissolved. Add bouillon to stuffing mixture. Toss with a fork until well mixed.
3. Wash mushrooms; pat dry on paper towels. Remove stems from mushrooms; reserve for another use.
4. Place butter or margarine in a glass baking cup. Microwave at 100% (HIGH) 45 seconds or until melted. Dip mushrooms in butter or margarine. Fill mushrooms with stuffing mixture. Arrange mushrooms in a circle on a 12-inch-round microwave platter, propping mushrooms up along edge of plate. Drizzle with any remaining butter or margarine. Garnish with pimento strips.
5. Microwave at 100% (HIGH) 4 to 5 minutes or until heated through; give platter a half turn after 2 minutes. Remove any smaller mushrooms as soon as they are cooked; keep warm. Continue microwaving remaining mushrooms. Makes 4 servings.

Nut Nibblers

2 tablespoons butter or margarine
1 teaspoon celery salt
1 teaspoon chili powder
1 teaspoon onion powder
3-1/2 cups mixed pecan halves, cashews, almonds
    (13 oz.)

1. In a 1-cup glass measuring cup, combine butter or margarine, celery salt, chili powder and onion powder. Microwave at 100% (HIGH) 30 seconds or until butter or margarine melts.
2. Place nuts in a 12" x 7" baking dish. Stir butter or margarine mixture; pour over nuts. Toss until coated thoroughly. Microwave at 30% (MEDIUM LOW) 20 minutes or until toasted; stir every 7 minutes. Cool completely. Store in a plastic bag or airtight container. Makes 3 cups.

How to Make Spinach-Stuffed Appetizer Oysters

1/Pierce oysters with a large fork to break membrane. This prevents oysters from bursting during microwaving.

2/Dip oysters in melted butter or margarine mixture. Rinse and reuse oyster shells. Place butter-dipped oysters in rinsed oyster shells.

Bacon-Nut-Stuffed Artichokes

8 bacon slices
1/2 cup chopped onion
1/2 cup chopped pecans, toasted
2/3 cup seasoned dry bread crumbs
2 tablespoons dry white wine
2 (14-oz.) cans artichoke bottoms, drained (about 12 bottoms)
3 tablespoons butter or margarine
1 teaspoon lemon juice

To garnish:
Pecan halves

1. Place bacon on a microwave rack in a 12-inch-square microwave baker. Cover bacon with a white paper towel. Microwave at 100% (HIGH) 7 to 9 minutes or until crisp; give dish a half turn after 4 minutes. Remove bacon. Drain on paper towels; crumble drained bacon.
2. Remove rack from baking dish. Drain off all but 1/4 cup drippings. Add onion to baking dish. Microwave at 100% (HIGH) 3 to 4 minutes or until tender; stir once.
3. Add chopped pecans, bread crumbs, wine and crumbled bacon. Toss lightly to mix well.
4. Rinse artichoke bottoms; pat dry with paper towels. Place butter or margarine in a 1-1/2-cup bowl. Microwave at 100% (HIGH) 45 to 60 seconds or until melted. Stir in lemon juice.
5. Dip artichokes in butter or margarine mixture. Top artichokes with bacon mixture. Arrange in a circle in a 12-inch-square microwave baker. Drizzle with any remaining butter or margarine mixture. Garnish with pecan halves. Microwave at 100% (HIGH) 5 to 7 minutes or until heated through; give dish a half turn after 3 minutes. Makes 6 servings.

Spinach-Stuffed Appetizer Oysters

1/2 (12-oz.) pkg. frozen spinach soufflé
3 tablespoons seasoned dry bread crumbs
3 tablespoons grated Parmesan cheese
1 tablespoon butter or margarine
1/2 teaspoon lemon juice
8 fresh shucked oysters, drained

To garnish:
Pimento strips

1. Remove frozen soufflé from package, Cut in half with a sharp knife. Return 1/2 of soufflé to freezer. Place remaining 1/2 of frozen soufflé in a 1-quart bowl. Microwave at 30% (MEDIUM LOW) 3 minutes or until thawed; break up with a fork after 1-1/2 minutes. Let stand 3 minutes. Stir bread crumbs and Parmesan cheese into soufflé.
2. Place butter or margarine in a glass baking cup. Microwave at 100% (HIGH) 45 seconds or until melted. Stir in lemon juice.
3. Pat oysters dry on paper towels. Pierce with a large fork. Dip oysters in melted butter or margarine mixture; place in rinsed shells. Top oysters with spinach mixture. Drizzle with any remaining butter or margarine mixture.
4. Arrange in a circle on a 12-inch-round microwave platter. Top oysters with pimento strips. Microwave at 50% (MEDIUM) 4 to 5 minutes or until heated through; give platter a half turn after 2 minutes. Let stand 1 minute before serving. Makes 4 servings.

Chicken-Liver & Bacon Appetizers (Rumaki)

4 oz. chicken livers
2 tablespoons soy sauce
1 tablespoon dry sherry
1 garlic clove, minced
1 teaspoon grated fresh gingerroot
1/2 (8-oz.) can water chestnuts, drained
9 bacon slices

1. Cut chicken livers in 1-inch pieces. Pierce with a large fork. In a medium bowl, combine soy sauce, sherry, garlic and gingerroot. Place chicken livers in marinade. Mix well. Cover and marinate at room temperature 30 minutes.
2. Cut water chestnuts in half. Cut bacon slices in half crosswise. Remove chicken livers from marinade; drain on paper towels. Place bacon on a rack in a 12-inch-square microwave baker. Cover with white paper towels. Microwave at 100% (HIGH) 4 minutes or until bacon is partially cooked. Drain off fat from dish.
3. Place 1 piece of water chestnut and 1 piece of chicken liver on 1 half-slice of bacon. Roll up and secure with a wooden pick. Place on rack in same baker. Repeat with remaining water chestnuts, chicken livers and bacon.
4. Microwave at 100% (HIGH) 5-1/2 to 6-1/2 minutes or until bacon is crisp and liver is slightly pink in center. Turn livers over and rearrange once during cooking. Makes 18 pieces.

Variation
To cook 8 ounces of chicken livers, cook in 2 batches using directions above. Do not attempt to microwave 36 Rumaki at once.

Tomato Tang

2 (12-oz.) cans vegetable-tomato juice cocktail (3 cups)
1 (14-1/2-oz.) can beef broth
1 tablespoon lemon juice
1 teaspoon Worcestershire sauce
1 teaspoon prepared horseradish
Dash hot-pepper sauce

To garnish:
6 thin lemon slices, halved, with a parsley sprig on each

1. In a deep 2-quart casserole with lid, combine vegetable-tomato juice cocktail, beef broth, lemon juice, Worcestershire sauce, horseradish and hot-pepper sauce. Cover. Microwave at 100% (HIGH) 8 to 10 minutes or until mixture is boiling.
2. Stir. Cover. Microwave at 30% (MEDIUM LOW) 10 to 12 minutes to blend flavors; stir once. Garnish with lemon slices topped with parsley sprigs. Makes 4 servings.

Bacon-Olive Cracker Melts

1 (5-oz.) jar process-cheese spread
1/4 cup chopped pimento-stuffed green olives
3 bacon slices, crisp-cooked, crumbled
Dash red (cayenne) pepper
24 Melba-toast rounds or crackers

To garnish:
Olive slices, if desired

1. Place cheese spread in a 1-quart bowl. Microwave at 10% (LOW) 1 minute or until soft. Stir in olives, bacon and cayenne.
2. Place Melba toast or crackers in a circle on a round 12-inch microwave platter. Spread about 1 teaspoon cheese mixture on each cracker. Garnish each cracker with an olive slice, if desired.
3. Microwave at 100% (HIGH) 45 to 60 seconds or until cheese melts; give plate a half turn after 30 seconds. Makes 24 appetizers.

Dilly Ham Dip

1 (8-oz.) pkg. cream cheese
1 tablespoon milk
1 teaspoon Worcestershire sauce
2 tablespoons chopped green onion
Dash freshly ground pepper
3 tablespoons prepared sandwich spread
1 cup finely chopped cooked ham
3 tablespoons chopped dill pickle, drained
2 teaspoons prepared mustard

To garnish:
Green- and red-bell pepper strips
Parsley sprig

To serve:
Fresh vegetables or crackers

1. Place cream cheese in a 1-1/2-quart bowl. Microwave at 10% (LOW) 1-1/2 to 2 minutes or until softened.
2. Add milk, Worcestershire sauce, green onion and pepper. Beat with an electric mixer on medium speed until blended.
3. Stir in sandwich spread, ham, dill pickle and mustard. Spoon into a 9-inch serving dish. Cover with vented plastic wrap. Microwave at 70% (MEDIUM HIGH) 3 to 3-1/2 minutes or until heated through; stir twice. Garnish with pepper strips and parsley. Serve warm with fresh vegetables or crackers as dippers. Makes 2 cups.

Clockwise from top left: Tomato Tang; Dilly Ham Dip; Curried-Chicken Snack Sandwiches, page 10; Bacon-Olive Cracker Melts; Chicken-Liver & Bacon Appetizers

Soups & Sauces

Q. What are the advantages of cooking soups and sauces in the microwave?

A. Individual servings of soup can be heated in moments in mugs or bowls. Big batches of soup made on top of the range can be frozen in family-size portions and reheated in the microwave. Sauces don't need to be stirred constantly as they do on top of the range. And there's an added bonus—they don't stick to the dish!

Q. Which soups or sauces do not cook satisfactorily in the microwave?

A. Dried-bean and pea soups can be cooked successfully in the microwave, but not much time is saved. When a sauce depends on eggs for thickening, it is difficult to prevent it from curdling.

Q. How are soups and sauces cooked in the microwave?

A. These recipes use a range of microwave-cooking techniques. Most soups made from scratch come to boiling at 100% (HIGH) and then simmer at 30% (MEDIUM LOW). Canned soups and soup mixes generally heat very quickly at 100% (HIGH). For maximum thickness, the *roux*, the butter and flour mixture, for sauces should be

cooked for 30 seconds at 100% (HIGH) before the liquid is added. Hollandaise sauce benefits from an ingenious hot-water bath that keeps the outside portion of the sauce from curdling before the center is warm.

Q. How do you know when soups and sauces are done?

A. Soups should be at least 170F (75C) before serving. Be sure to stir soups before serving to help equalize the temperature throughout the soup. Remember that soups bubble around the edges long before the center is hot. Thickened sauces also start to bubble at the edges partway through the cooking time. Don't stop cooking then! Stir the sauce often with a whisk to prevent lumping; continue cooking according to the recipe until the sauce is thickened and smooth.

Q. Are any special utensils needed to cook soups and sauces in the microwave?

A. For many of the start-from-scratch soups, use a 4-quart casserole. This is quite large by conventional standards, but allows plenty of room for boiling and stirring. Large measuring cups in the 1- or 2-quart sizes are handy for mixing, cooking, pouring and storing sauces.

How to Reheat Frozen Soup

1/Place the frozen block of soup in a casserole. Cover. Microwave until soup is partially thawed; break apart soup with a fork to complete thawing.

2/After soup is thawed, heat to serving temperature; stir occasionally. Top soups with croutons, chopped ham, chopped herbs or other garnishes.

Spicy All-Purpose Tomato Sauce, page 18

Shortcut Minestrone

1 lb. ground beef
1 cup chopped onion
1/2 cup chopped green bell pepper
1 (16-oz.) can tomatoes
1 (16-oz.) jar Italian cooking sauce (2 cups)
1 cup Chianti wine
1 (15-1/2-oz.) can chili beans with gravy
1/2 cup spaghetti, broken in 1-inch pieces
2 oz. thinly sliced pepperoni
1 teaspoon dried leaf basil

To garnish:
Croutons, if desired
Grated Parmesan cheese, if desired

1. In a deep 3-quart casserole with lid, combine ground beef, onion and green pepper. Microwave at 100% (HIGH) 5 to 6 minutes or until meat is no longer pink and vegetables are tender; stir after 2 minutes. Drain off fat.
2. Chop tomatoes, reserving juice. Stir in cooking sauce, chopped tomatoes with juice, wine, beans with gravy, spaghetti, pepperoni and basil. Cover. Microwave at 100% (HIGH) 10 minutes or until boiling. Stir well. Cover.
3. Microwave at 30% (MEDIUM LOW) 35 minutes or until spaghetti is tender; stir twice. To serve, top each serving with croutons and grated Parmesan cheese, if desired. Makes 6 servings.

Lazy-Day Vichyssoise

1 (9-oz.) pkg. frozen small onions with cream sauce
2/3 cup water
1 tablespoon chicken-bouillon granules
1 tablespoon butter or margarine
1 cup milk
3/4 cup instant mashed-potato buds
1/2 cup whipping cream

To garnish:
Chopped chives

1. In a deep 1-quart casserole with lid, combine frozen onions, water, bouillon granules and butter or margarine. Cover. Microwave at 100% (HIGH) 3 minutes. Stir until sauce is smooth. Stir in milk. Cover. Microwave at 100% (HIGH) 4 minutes or until onions are tender. Stir in potato buds.
2. In a blender or food processor with a steel blade, process mixture until smooth. Process in 2 batches, if necessary. Stir in whipping cream. Press mixture through a fine sieve, if desired. Cover and refrigerate 8 hours or overnight.
3. Serve icy cold in small bowls or icers. Top with chives. Makes 3 to 4 servings.

French Onion Soup

6 tablespoons butter or margarine
4 medium onions, thinly sliced (4 cups)
2 teaspoons all-purpose flour
1 tablespoon sugar
1 teaspoon dry mustard
2 (10-3/4-oz.) cans condensed chicken broth
1/4 cup dry white wine
2 teaspoons Worcestershire sauce
1 cup croutons
1/4 cup grated Parmesan cheese
1 cup shredded mozzarella cheese (4 oz.)

1. Place butter or margarine in a deep 3-quart casserole. Microwave butter or margarine at 100% (HIGH) 1-1/2 minutes or until melted. Stir in onions. Microwave at 100% (HIGH) 25 to 30 minutes or until onions are browned and caramelized; stir every 5 minutes.
2. Stir in flour, sugar and mustard; microwave at 100% (HIGH) 2 minutes or until mixture bubbles. Gradually stir in broth, wine and Worcestershire sauce. Microwave at 100% (HIGH) 9 to 10 minutes or until mixture thickens slightly and bubbles; stir every 3 minutes.
3. Ladle into 4 bowls. Top each serving with croutons. Sprinkle with Parmesan cheese and mozzarella cheese. Microwave at 100% (HIGH) 2 to 2-1/2 minutes or just until cheese melts; turn bowls after 1 minute. Makes 4 servings.

French Onion Soup

Split Pea Soup

8 oz. dried split peas (about 1-1/4 cups)
8 oz. bulk pork sausage
1/2 cup chopped onion
1/2 cup chopped celery
5 cups chicken broth
1 teaspoon fennel seed

To garnish:
Chopped ham
Croutons
Chopped parsley

1. Rinse and drain split peas; set aside. In a deep 4-quart casserole with lid, combine sausage, onion and celery. Microwave at 100% (HIGH) 5 to 7 minutes or until sausage is no longer pink; stir after 3 minutes. Drain off fat.
2. Stir in peas, broth and fennel seed; cover. Microwave at 100% (HIGH) 22 to 25 minutes. Stir and cover. Microwave at 30% (MEDIUM LOW) 50 to 60 minutes or until peas are tender; stir occasionally. Skim off excess fat. Garnish with chopped ham, croutons and parsley. Makes 4 servings.

Spicy All-Purpose Tomato Sauce

2 tablespoons olive oil
1/4 cup chopped onion
1/4 cup chopped green bell pepper
1/4 cup chopped celery
2 (16-oz.) cans tomatoes, drained, chopped (1-2/3 cups)
2 teaspoons brown sugar
1/4 teaspoon salt
1/4 teaspoon dried leaf oregano
1/4 teaspoon dried leaf basil
1/8 teaspoon garlic powder

1. In a deep 1-1/2-quart casserole with lid, combine olive oil, onion, green pepper and celery. Microwave at 100% (HIGH) 3 minutes or until vegetables are tender; stir after 1-1/2 minutes.
2. Stir in tomatoes, brown sugar, salt, oregano, basil and garlic powder. Cover. Microwave at 100% (HIGH) 5 minutes or until mixture boils. Stir well; cover. Microwave at 30% (MEDIUM LOW) 15 to 20 minutes or until sauce reaches desired consistency; stir after 10 minutes. Makes 1-1/2 cups.

Old-Fashioned Vegetable Soup

2 lb. beef neck bones
1 large onion, chopped
2 celery stalks, chopped
1 bay leaf
1 tablespoon Worcestershire sauce
1 (12-oz.) can vegetable-tomato juice cocktail
1 (28-oz.) can tomatoes, chopped (1-1/2 cups)
1 (10-oz.) pkg. frozen mixed vegetables (2 cups)

1. In a 4-quart casserole with lid, place neck bones, meaty-side down. Add onion, celery, bay leaf and Worcestershire sauce. Pour in vegetable-tomato juice cocktail and tomatoes. Cover.
2. Microwave at 100% (HIGH) 15 minutes or until boiling. Microwave at 30% (MEDIUM LOW) 1-1/2 hours or until meat is tender; stir twice. Let stand covered 20 minutes. Remove bones. Cover bones tightly; set aside.
3. Add mixed vegetables to liquid in casserole. Break apart vegetables with a large fork. Cover. Microwave at 100% (HIGH) 15 minutes or until vegetables are almost tender.
4. While vegetables are cooking, cut meat from bones; discard bones. Stir meat into soup. Cover. Microwave at 100% (HIGH) 10 minutes or until heated through. Skim off excess fat. Makes 4 servings.

Quick & Creamy Chicken Chowder

1 (10-3/4-oz.) can condensed cream of chicken soup
1-1/2 soup cans milk
1 (10-oz.) pkg. frozen broccoli, carrots and pasta twists with sauce cubes
1/8 teaspoon rubbed sage
1 cup diced cooked or canned chicken

To garnish:
Chopped watercress or parsley

1. In a deep 2-quart casserole with lid, combine soup and milk. Whisk until smooth. Stir in frozen vegetables with sauce cubes and sage. Cover.
2. Microwave at 100% (HIGH) 5 minutes. Stir until sauce cubes dissolve. Add chicken. Cover. Microwave at 100% (HIGH) 10 to 12 minutes or until heated through; stir after 5 minutes. Let stand, covered, 2 minutes.
3. Stir before serving. Garnish each serving with watercress or parsley. Makes 3 to 4 servings.

How to Make No-Fail Hollandaise Sauce

1/In a blender container, combine egg yolks, lemon juice, salt and white pepper.

2/Blend egg yolks and lemon juice until frothy. Then with blender running at high speed, slowly pour in melted butter or margarine. Blend until sauce is thick and creamy.

3/Pour sauce into a glass measuring cup or sauce boat. Set sauce in a large bowl. Pour hot water into bowl. This water bath helps keep sauce from curdling.

4/Microwave sauce just until warm—it will curdle if it becomes hot. Spoon sauce over omelets, Eggs Benedict, vegetables, fish or poultry dishes.

No-Fail Hollandaise Sauce

3 egg yolks
2 tablespoons lemon juice
Dash salt
Dash white pepper
1/2 cup butter or margarine, cut in pieces
1/4 teaspoon dried leaf tarragon
1/4 teaspoon grated fresh lemon peel

1. In a blender container, combine egg yolks, lemon juice, salt and pepper. Cover and blend at low speed until frothy. Place butter or margarine in a 2-cup glass measuring cup. Microwave at 100% (HIGH) 1 to 1-1/2 minutes or until melted.
2. With blender at high speed, slowly pour in melted butter or margarine, blending constantly until mixture is very thick. Stir in tarragon and lemon peel.
3. To warm, pour into same glass measuring cup or a sauce boat; set in bowl of hot water. The hot water should be at the same level as the sauce. Microwave at 30% (MEDIUM LOW) 5 minutes, or until warm; stir every 2 minutes. Stir before serving. Cover and refrigerate any leftover sauce. Makes 1 cup.

Curried Asparagus Bisque

2 tablespoons butter or margarine
1/4 cup chopped onion
1/2 teaspoon celery salt
1 teaspoon curry powder
1 (10-3/4-oz.) can condensed chicken broth
1 (8-oz.) pkg. frozen cut asparagus
1-1/2 teaspoons lemon juice
1/2 cup plain yogurt

To garnish:
1/2 avocado, sliced
1/4 cup plain yogurt
Chopped chives or red caviar

1. Place butter or margarine in a deep 2-quart casserole. Microwave at 100% (HIGH) 30 seconds or until melted. Add onion. Microwave at 100% (HIGH) 2 to 2-1/2 minutes or until tender.
2. Stir in celery salt and curry powder. Stir in chicken broth. Add asparagus; cover. Microwave at 100% (HIGH) 7 to 8 minutes or until tender.
3. Stir in lemon juice. In a blender or food processor with a steel blade, process mixture until smooth. Process in 2 batches, if necessary.
4. In same casserole, blend yogurt and a little hot soup mixture. Gradually blend in remaining hot soup. Cover and refrigerate 8 hours or overnight. Serve icy cold in small bowls or icers. Top each serving with a fan of avocado slices, a dollop of yogurt and a sprinkling of chives or caviar. Makes 4 servings.

Swiss Corn Chowder

1 (10-3/4-oz.) can condensed cream of onion soup
1-1/2 soup cans milk
1 (8-3/4-oz.) can cream-style corn
1 (7-oz.) can whole-kernel corn
1/4 cup chopped pimento
1/2 cup shredded Swiss cheese (2 oz.)

1. In a deep 2-quart casserole with lid, whisk together soup, milk and cream-style corn. Stir in whole-kernel corn with liquid and pimento. Cover.
2. Microwave at 100% (HIGH) 10 minutes or until heated through; stir after 5 minutes. Stir in cheese. Microwave, uncovered, at 70% (MEDIUM HIGH) 2 minutes or until cheese is melted; stir after 1 minute. Makes 4 servings.

Tuna Chowder Florentine

1 (9-oz.) pkg. frozen creamed spinach in a pouch
2 cups milk
1 (6-1/2-oz.) can water-pack tuna, drained, broken up
2 hard-cooked eggs, chopped
2 tablespoons chopped pimento
2 teaspoons snipped chives
2 teaspoons Dijon-style mustard
1 teaspoon lemon juice

To garnish:
1 hard-cooked egg, sliced
Paprika

1. Remove creamed spinach from pouch. Place in a deep 2-quart casserole with lid. Cover. Microwave at 100% (HIGH) 7 minutes. Stir in milk. Stir in tuna, eggs, pimento, chives, mustard and lemon juice. Cover.
2. Microwave at 100% (HIGH) 8 minutes or until hot; stir after 4 minutes. Garnish with hard-cooked egg; sprinkle with paprika. Makes 4 servings.

Oriental Chicken Soup

1 boneless chicken breast
2 (14-1/2-oz.) cans chicken broth
1/4 cup thinly sliced celery
1/4 cup thinly sliced green onions
2 tablespoons dry sherry
1/2 cup chopped watercress leaves

1. Remove skin from chicken breast, if necessary. Cut chicken into 1-inch slivers; set aside. Pour broth into a deep 2-quart casserole with lid. Cover. Microwave at 100% (HIGH) 8 to 10 minutes or until boiling.
2. Add chicken pieces. Cover. Microwave at 100% (HIGH) 3 to 4 minutes or until chicken is almost done. Add celery, green onions and sherry. Microwave at 100% (HIGH) 3 to 5 minutes or until vegetables are crisp-tender.
3. Divide watercress leaves among 4 to 6 soup cups. Pour in hot soup. Makes 4 to 6 servings

Tuna Chowder Florentine

Meats

Q. What are the advantages of cooking meat in the microwave?

A. Most meats can be cooked in the microwave with a good saving of time. In addition, there are fewer preparation dishes and no baked-on mess to clean up.

Q. What are the disadvantages of cooking meat in the microwave?

A. A few meats, such as pot roast, take almost as long to cook in the microwave as they would conventionally. In addition, these meats usually require more attention from the cook when the microwave is used. Unless the microwave is the only cooking device available, it may be less trouble to cook these recipes conventionally. Roasts may be cooked considerably faster in the microwave. But they also require more attention and should be a uniform and compact shape. When considering cost, time and convenience, many cooks may feel more comfortable cooking them conventionally.

Q. Which meats do not cook satisfactorily in the microwave?

A. Meats cannot be deep-fried in the microwave. Extra-large roasts and pot roasts are difficult to cook in the microwave because it is not easy to achieve an even doneness.

Q. How are meats cooked in the microwave?

A. Generally, meats are divided into the same two categories used in conventional cooking—meats requiring *moist-heat* cooking and those using *dry-heat* cooking. Most meats requiring moist heat in conventional cooking also require moist heat in microwave cooking. The same holds true for dry-heat microwave cooking. Ham is the most notable exception. It is cooked with moist heat in the microwave to prevent it from drying out.

Q. How do you know when meat is done?

A. Doneness tests are given with each type of basic meat recipe. A microwave meat thermometer is especially helpful when checking the doneness of roasts. Pot roasts should be fork-tender, just as they are when cooked conventionally. A small slit in the center of a chop will reveal if the meat is pink. Meat, and all foods, continue cooking during the standing time given in the recipe.

Q. How can I make meat cooked in the microwave look brown?

A. This is really only a problem for small, thin cuts, such as chops, which cook quickly. You can use a sauce or crumb coating to cover the meat. Or, sprinkle it sparingly with one of the color-enhancing products available. Or, use a flavoring such as paprika. The browning skillet has eliminated this problem with steaks, burgers and chops. With cuts requiring longer cooking, the opposite problem arises. You have to be careful to avoid overbrowning. Follow the cooking times given in the recipes. If the meat is cooked in liquid, be sure it is under the liquid throughout cooking. Meat cooked in the microwave darkens quickly after cooking. Keep meat closely covered after taking it from the oven. This includes sliced meat.

Q. How can favorite conventional recipes be converted for microwave cooking?

A. Check recipes given here for the same type of recipe you wish to make. Most recipes can be converted successfully for microwave cooking.

Q. What about cooking main-dish convenience foods in the microwave?

A. Many convenience foods can be microwaved. Check the packages for the manufacturers' instructions. The packaging material of frozen foods is changing rapidly to enable more foods to be cooked in original packaging in the microwave.

Q. How do you defrost meat in the microwave?

A. Microwave defrosting can be extremely successful if you use two power levels. Start defrosting at 30% (MEDIUM LOW) then use 10% (LOW) to finish the process.

Q. Are there any special utensils needed to cook meats in the microwave?

A. Many meats requiring dry-heat cooking, such as roasts and chops, are cooked on a microwave rack in a baking dish. The rack holds the meat out of the juices so it will not stew. Most microwave racks are made from special plastic or ceramic. Inverted saucers can be used to simulate a rack. A browning skillet is essential for searing cuts like steaks or chops that cook in a short time.

Easy Paella, page 25

How to Make Pot Roast with Vegetables

1/Slash fat edges of roast with a sharp knife. This helps to keep meat flat during cooking. Cut roast in serving-size pieces. This makes meat easier to arrange in casserole and helps meat cook more evenly.

2/Pierce pieces deeply all over on both sides with a large fork. This has the same effect as pounding other cuts of meat. It makes pot roast more tender and juicy.

Easy Swiss Steak

1-1/2 lb. beef round steak, 1/2 inch thick
3 tablespoons all-purpose flour
1 (8-oz.) can tomato sauce
1 cup water
1 (1-oz.) envelope Swiss-steak seasoning mix

1. Slash fat edges of meat. Cut meat in 5 or 6 pieces. Coat meat with flour. With a meat mallet, pound meat until it is 1/4 inch thick.
2. In a 3-quart casserole with lid, mix tomato sauce, water and Swiss-steak seasoning mix. Add steak pieces, making sure all meat is covered by liquid. Cover and let stand 10 minutes.
3. Microwave at 100% (HIGH) 10 minutes. Microwave at 30% (MEDIUM LOW) 30 minutes. Turn steak over; give casserole a half turn. Microwave at 30% (MEDIUM LOW) 20 minutes. Let stand, covered, 10 minutes. Meat is done when it can be easily pierced with a fork. Makes 5 to 6 servings.

Meat Loaf

1 lb. ground beef chuck
1 egg
1/4 cup quick-cooking rolled oats
2 tablespoons chopped onion
1 (8-oz.) can tomato sauce
1/4 teaspoon dried leaf thyme
1/4 teaspoon dried leaf marjoram
1/2 teaspoon celery salt
1 tablespoon brown sugar
1 teaspoon Worcestershire sauce
1 teaspoon prepared mustard

1. In a medium bowl, thoroughly combine meat, egg, oats, onion, 1/2 of tomato sauce, thyme, marjoram and celery salt. Press meat mixture into a loaf in a 9" x 5" loaf dish; shape loaf so meat does not touch sides of dish.
2. Cover with waxed paper. Microwave at 100% (HIGH) 5 minutes. Pour off juices.
3. Stir brown sugar, Worcestershire sauce and mustard into remaining tomato sauce. Spoon tomato glaze over loaf, coating entire top and sides. Give dish a half turn. Cover with waxed paper. Microwave at 30% (MEDIUM LOW) 17 to 20 minutes or until a microwave meat thermometer inserted in center of loaf registers 170F (75C) or until meat in center is only slightly pink.
4. Cover with foil; let stand 5 minutes. Temperature will rise about 10F (5C) during standing time. Makes 4 servings.

Pot Roast with Vegetables

2 lb. beef chuck roast, about 1-1/4 to 1-1/2 inches thick
1 teaspoon dried leaf thyme
1 cup unsweetened apple juice
1 to 1-1/2 cups beef broth
2 tablespoons vinegar
2 potatoes, cut up (2 cups)
4 carrots, cut up (2 cups)
2 medium onions, cut up

1. Trim off large fat edges from roast. Slash remaining fat edges of roast at 1-inch intervals. Cut in 4 serving pieces. Pierce pieces deeply all over on both sides with a large fork. Place in a deep 3-quart casserole with lid; pieces should lie flat. Sprinkle with thyme.
2. Combine apple juice, 1 cup beef broth and vinegar in a medium bowl or glass measuring cup. Pour over roast. Roast must be completely covered with liquid to cook evenly. Add additional broth to cover, if necessary. If time permits, cover meat and let marinate several hours or overnight in the refrigerator. This gives added tenderness and flavor.
3. Cover roast with lid. Microwave at 100% (HIGH) 10 minutes. Microwave at 30% (MEDIUM LOW) 30 minutes. Turn pieces of roast over. Add vegetables and cover. Other vegetables can be substituted, such as turnips, celery, rutabaga and parsnips.
4. Microwave at 30% (MEDIUM LOW) 60 to 75 minutes. Turn top vegetables over in broth. Let stand, covered, 20 minutes. Standing time is very important; do not omit this step. Meat is done when it can be easily pieced with a fork. Vegetables should be tender when pierced with a fork. Makes 4 servings.

Easy Paella

4 bacon slices
2 (10-oz.) pkgs. frozen Spanish-style rice
6 tablespoons water
1 cup cubed, cooked pork or ham (4 oz.)
1 (4-1/2-oz.) can large shrimp, drained
1 large tomato, cut in wedges

1. Place bacon in a 2-quart casserole with lid. Cover with white paper towels. Microwave at 100% (HIGH) 4 minutes or until crisp. Remove bacon from casserole, leaving drippings in casserole. Drain bacon on paper towels. Crumble drained bacon; set aside.
2. Stir contents of seasoning pouch from rice into bacon drippings in casserole. Stir in water. Add frozen rice. Cover. Microwave at 100% (HIGH) 6 minutes.
3. Stir in pork or ham, shrimp and tomato wedges; cover. Microwave at 100% (HIGH) 8 minutes or until rice is tender and meat is heated through. Top with crumbled bacon. Makes 4 to 6 servings.

Cutlets

1 egg
1 tablespoon water
2 tablespoons all-purpose flour
3/4 cup dry seasoned bread crumbs
1/2 teaspoon dried leaf marjoram
1 tablespoon dried parsley flakes
4 (4- to 5-oz.) pork or veal cutlets, pounded
3 tablespoons vegetable oil

1. In a pie plate, whisk egg and water until frothy. Place flour in a pie plate or on waxed paper. In another pie plate or on waxed paper, mix bread crumbs, marjoram and parsley flakes. Coat cutlets on both sides with flour. Dip both sides in egg mixture, then in crumb mixture, coating generously. Press crumb mixture into meat with fingers.
2. Preheat a 10-inch microwave browning skillet at 100% (HIGH) 4 minutes. Add oil to hot browning skillet. Using hot pads, tilt skillet to coat evenly with oil. Quickly add cutlets. Microwave at 100% (HIGH) 3-1/2 minutes.
3. Turn cutlets over. Microwave at 100% (HIGH) 3-1/2 minutes or until done. Let stand 1 minute. Meat should no longer be pink when cut. Makes 4 servings.

Chinese Tacos

1 lb. ground beef or pork
1/4 cup chopped green onions
1/4 cup chopped water chestnuts
2 teaspoons cornstarch
2 tablespoons soy sauce
1 teaspoon vinegar
1/2 teaspoon dry mustard
1/2 teaspoon ground ginger
1/2 teaspoon beef-bouillon granules
1/3 cup water
5 or 6 large crisp iceberg-lettuce leaves
1 (3-oz.) can fried rice noodles or chow mein noodles

1. Crumble meat into a deep 2-quart casserole. Add green onions. Cover with waxed paper. Microwave at 100% (HIGH) 5 minutes or until meat is no longer pink; stir twice. Pour off juices. Add water chestnuts.
2. In a small bowl, mix cornstarch, soy sauce and vinegar. Stir in dry mustard and ginger until smooth. Stir into meat mixture; mix well. Add bouillon granules and water; stir until well mixed. Cover. Microwave at 100% (HIGH) 3 minutes or until thickened and bubbly; stir once.
3. To serve, spoon meat mixture into center of lettuce leaves. Top with noodles. Fold up, envelope-style, to eat. Serve with additional soy sauce. Makes 5 to 6 servings.

Speedy Stew

1 lb. beef chuck, or lamb, pork or veal shoulder
2-2/3 cups water
1 (1.5-oz.) envelope seasoning mix for stew
1 (24-oz.) pkg. frozen stew vegetables
1 cup frozen green peas
3 tablespoons all-purpose flour
1/3 cup water

1. Pierce meat deeply on all sides with a large fork. Cut into 1-inch cubes. Place meat in a deep 3-quart casserole with lid. Add 2-2/3 cups water and seasoning mix. Mix well, making sure meat is covered by liquid. Cover. Microwave at 100% (HIGH) 10 minutes. Stir; cover. Microwave at 30% (MEDIUM LOW) 30 minutes.
2. Stir in frozen stew vegetables, making sure meat is still covered by liquid. Cover. Microwave at 30% (MEDIUM LOW) 45 minutes or until meat and vegetables are almost tender.
3. Stir in peas; mix well. Cover. Microwave at 30% (MEDIUM LOW) 15 minutes or until meat and vegetables are tender. Meat is done when it can be easily pieced with a fork. Vegetables should be tender when pierced with a fork. Let stand, covered, 10 minutes.
4. Shake together flour and water in a screw-top jar. Stir into stew. Microwave, uncovered, at 100% (HIGH) 2 to 3 minutes or until thickened and bubbly; stir 3 times. Makes 3 to 4 servings.

Simmered Barbecued Ribs

3 to 3-1/2 lb. pork loin back ribs or beef short ribs, 2-1/2 inches long and 1/2 to 1 inch thick
1 large onion, sliced, separated into rings
1 large bay leaf
2 (12-oz.) cans beer, room temperature
2 tablespoons Worcestershire sauce
2-1/2 cups bottled barbecue sauce

1. Cut pork ribs into 2-rib portions. Cut thick beef short ribs in half lengthwise. Pierce ribs all over with a large fork. Place, bone-side up, in a deep 4-quart casserole with lid. Add onion and bay leaf. Pour in beer and Worcestershire sauce.

2. Cover and microwave at 100% (HIGH) 10 minutes. Microwave at 30% (MEDIUM LOW) 30 minutes. Rearrange ribs, bringing ribs in center of casserole to outside edge. Be sure ribs are bone-side up and meaty side is under liquid. Cover. Microwave at 30% (MEDIUM LOW) 60 to 75 minutes.
3. Let ribs stand, covered, 20 minutes. Meat is done when it can be easily pierced with a fork. Pour off pan juices from casserole. Turn ribs meaty-side up. Pour barbecue sauce over ribs, coating well. Cover. Microwave at 30% (MEDIUM LOW) 10 minutes or until heated through. Serve ribs with onion and sauce. Makes 3 to 4 servings.

New England Boiled Dinner

2-1/2 to 3 lb. boneless corned-beef brisket
4 cups ginger ale
2 boiling potatoes, cut up (2 cups)
2 medium onions, cut up
2 medium carrots, cut up
1/2 large rutabaga, peeled, cubed
1/2 small cabbage, cut in 4 wedges

1. Slash fat edges of roast at 1-inch intervals. Score fat on top and bottom of roast. Place roast, fat-side down, in a floured roasting bag set in a deep 4-quart casserole. Choose the size roasting bag and baking dish that allows the meat to be as totally immersed in liquid as possible.
2. Add spices from corned-beef package, if any. Add ginger ale to cover roast. Tie roasting bag with string, leaving a 2-inch opening to vent steam. Microwave at 100% (HIGH) 10 minutes. Microwave at 30% (MEDIUM LOW) 30 minutes.
3. Carefully open roasting bag; turn roast over. Add potatoes, onions, carrots and rutabaga. Tie bag, leaving a 2-inch opening. Microwave at 30% (MEDIUM LOW) 60 minutes or until meat can be pierced with a fork with little resistance.
4. Open roasting bag; let steam escape. Add cabbage wedges. Tie roasting bag, leaving a 2-inch opening. Microwave at 30% (MEDIUM LOW) 30 minutes.
5. Allow steam to escape before testing for doneness. Meat is done when it can be easily pieced with a fork. When meat and vegetables are done, tie bag tightly. Let stand 20 minutes. Reserve cooking liquid. Carve meat in thin slices diagonally across the grain. Arrange on a warm serving platter with vegetables. Refrigerate any leftover corned beef and vegetables in cooking liquid. Makes 4 servings.

How to Make Creamy Onion-Smothered Chops

1/Place coated chops in a deep casserole. Whisk onion soup, milk, bouillon granules, steak sauce and any remaining flour mixture until smooth.

2/Top chops with onion rings. Arrange chops in casserole so thin portion is toward center and thicker loin portion is to outside.

3/Pour sauce mixture over chops and onion. Make sure all chops are coated with sauce. Partway through cooking time, chops are turned over and pushed back under sauce.

4/After cooking and standing, chops should be tender when pierced with a fork. Serve chops and pan gravy over mashed potatoes, noodles or rice. Garnish with parsley.

Creamy Onion-Smothered Chops

4 (4- to 6-oz.) pork loin chops, 1/2 inch thick
3 tablespoons all-purpose flour
1 teaspoon ground sage
1 large onion, sliced, separated into rings
1 (10-1/2-oz.) can condensed cream of onion soup
1/2 soup can milk
2 teaspoons beef-bouillon granules
2 tablespoons steak sauce

To garnish:
Chopped parsley

1. Slash fat edges of chops. In a shallow bowl, mix flour and sage. Coat meat with flour mixture. Place in a deep 2-quart casserole with lid, with tenderloin portion toward center of dish. Top with onion.
2. In a medium bowl, whisk soup, milk, bouillon granules, steak sauce and any remaining flour mixture until smooth. Pour mixture over chops, being sure to coat all chops. Cover and microwave 30 minutes at 30% (MEDIUM LOW). After 15 minutes, turn chops over and rearrange. Push chops under liquid. Cover and microwave for remaining time or until tender. Let stand, covered, 10 minutes. Chops are done when they have no pink color when cut in center.
3. Skim off any fat. Serve pan juices over chops. Garnish with parsley. Makes 4 servings.

Ham Ring

1/2 lb. ground cooked ham
1/2 lb. ground pork
1 egg
1/4 cup quick-cooking rolled oats
1/4 cup chili sauce
2 tablespoons chopped onion
2 tablespoons chopped green bell pepper
1/2 teaspoon dry mustard
1/4 cup chili sauce
1 tablespoon brown sugar
1/4 teaspoon dry mustard

1. In a medium bowl, thoroughly mix ham, pork, egg, oats, 1/4 cup chili sauce, onion, green pepper and 1/2 teaspoon dry mustard. Press into a ring in a 10-inch pie plate. Place a custard cup in center of pie plate. Shape ring so meat does not touch sides of dish or cup. Cover with waxed paper. Microwave at 100% (HIGH) 5 minutes.
2. Combine 1/4 cup chili sauce, brown sugar and 1/4 teaspoon mustard. Spread over ring, coating entire top and sides. Give dish a half turn. Microwave at 30% (MEDIUM LOW) 9 to 10 minutes. Cover with foil; let stand 5 minutes. A microwave meat thermometer inserted in center of ring should register 170F (75C). Makes 4 servings.

Spaghetti & Meat Sauce

1 lb. ground beef chuck
1 cup chopped onion
1/2 cup chopped green bell pepper
1 (16-oz.) can tomatoes
1 (8-oz.) can tomato sauce
1 (6-oz.) can tomato paste
1/4 cup water
1 bay leaf
2 teaspoons dried leaf oregano
1 teaspoon dried leaf basil
1 tablespoon Worcestershire sauce

To serve:
Hot cooked spaghetti
Grated Parmesan cheese

1. Crumble meat into a deep 3-quart casserole. Add onion and green pepper. Cover with waxed paper. Microwave at 100% (HIGH) 5 to 6 minutes or until meat is no longer pink; stir twice.
2. Pour off pan juices. Chop tomatoes, reserving juice. Stir in chopped tomatoes with juice, tomato sauce, tomato paste, water, bay leaf, oregano, basil and Worcestershire sauce. Cover. Microwave at 100% (HIGH) 10 minutes or until boiling.
3. Stir well. Microwave at 30% (MEDIUM LOW) 45 minutes or until sauce reaches desired consistency; stir occasionally. Discard bay leaf. Serve over hot cooked spaghetti. Sprinkle with Parmesan cheese. Makes 4 servings.

Easy Scalloped Potatoes & Ham

1 tablespoon butter or margarine
1/2 cup cheese-cracker crumbs or poppy-seed cracker crumbs
2 tablespoons butter or margarine
1/2 cup chopped celery
1/4 cup chopped onion
2 (10-oz.) pkgs. frozen creamed peas and potatoes
1-1/2 cups milk
1/4 cup chopped pimento
2 teaspoons prepared mustard
2 cups cooked ham (8 oz.), cut in 1/2-inch cubes

To garnish:
Watercress

1. In a small bowl, melt 1 tablespoon butter or margarine at 100% (HIGH) 30 seconds. Stir in cracker crumbs; set aside.
2. In a 2-quart casserole with lid, combine 2 tablespoons butter or margarine, celery and onion. Cover. Microwave at 100% (HIGH) 3 minutes; stir once.
3. Add frozen creamed peas and potatoes, milk, pimento and mustard. Cover. Microwave at 100% (HIGH) 6 minutes. Stir until sauce is smooth.
4. Stir in ham. Cover. Microwave at 100% (HIGH) 6 to 7 minutes or until heated through. Stir. Sprinkle buttered crumbs around edge of dish. Garnish with watercress. Makes 6 servings.

Poultry

The natural tenderness of poultry makes it ideal for fast microwave cooking. For a quick and easy dish for guests, try delicious *Chicken Cacciatore;* it takes little more than 30 minutes to prepare and cook.

Q. How is poultry cooked in the microwave?

A. Most poultry can be cooked at 100% (HIGH) because it is already tender meat. Larger whole poultry, such as turkeys, require a quick start at microwave 100% (HIGH) and then additional cooking at 50% (MEDIUM) to cook through evenly.

Q. Which poultry recipes do not cook satisfactorily in the microwave?

A. Deep-fried chicken cannot be cooked in the microwave. Turkeys over 12 pounds are difficult to cook evenly. Smaller whole turkeys weighing between 6 and 10 pounds can be cooked successfully in the microwave. Frozen, stuffed, whole turkeys should not be microwaved.

Q. How do you know when poultry is done?

A. Whole poultry is done when a microwave meat thermometer inserted between the leg and thigh registers 180F (80C). The temperature will rise very little, if any, during the standing time. For this reason, it is best to cook the poultry until it is done. As an additional test for doneness, the juices should run clear when whole poultry is cut between the leg and thigh, or when chicken or turkey pieces are pierced with a meat fork.

Q. Are any recipes given for using leftover turkey and chicken?

A. Try *Chicken à la King* or *Herbed-Chicken Pot Pies.* These and other delicious recipes use cooked turkey or chicken.

Q. Can poultry convenience foods be successfully cooked in the microwave?

A. Yes. Many frozen convenience foods, such as TV dinners or frozen chicken entrees in pouches, have microwave instructions on the package.

Q. Why do you rearrange chicken pieces during microwave cooking?

A. Chicken pieces are rearranged to promote even cooking. Move the center pieces of chicken to the outside of the dish and the ones from the outside edges to the center. Whole birds are turned over partway through the cooking time for the same reason.

Q. Will poultry brown in the microwave?

A. Poultry cooks so quickly in the microwave that the browning often needs a little assistance. Sauces and glazes enhance the appearance of whole birds. Chicken pieces can be cooked in sauce or crumbs for color.

Q. Is it safe to stuff whole birds that will be cooked in the microwave?

A. Stuffing must be cooked until it reaches a temperature of 165F (75C). This may mean overcooking the bird to reach this temperature. One way to overcome this problem is to select an airy bread stuffing rather than a heavy one using corn bread, for example. Do not pack the stuffing tightly into the bird. Always check the temperature of the stuffing before serving it.

Q. How can favorite conventional recipes be converted for microwave cooking?

A. Most poultry recipes can be adapted easily for microwave cooking. Start with basic recipes that can easily adapt.

Q. How do you defrost poultry in the microwave?

A. It is essential to place poultry on a microwave rack for defrosting so the bottom of the poultry does not start to cook in the juices. Poultry is defrosted first at 30% (MEDIUM LOW) and then at 10% (LOW). Finally, the poultry stands in cold water until it is completely defrosted.

Q. Are any special utensils needed for cooking poultry in the microwave?

A. Although you can use inverted saucers in the bottom of a baking dish to form a makeshift rack, it is handy to have a microwave rack. A microwave meat thermometer is useful to test doneness of whole chicken and turkey.

Roast Turkey, page 34

Chicken Aloha Crepes

3 cups cubed cooked chicken or turkey
1 (8-oz.) can pineapple chunks, drained
1/2 cup chopped macadamia nuts
1/2 cup chopped celery
1/4 cup chopped green onion
1/2 teaspoon celery salt
3/4 cup pineapple-flavored yogurt
3/4 cup mayonnaise
2 tablespoons dry white wine
1 teaspoon Dijon-style mustard
8 to 10 (6-inch) crepes

To garnish:
Toasted chopped macadamia nuts
Toasted coconut

1. In a large bowl, combine chicken or turkey, pineapple, macadamia nuts, celery, green onion and celery salt. In a small bowl, combine yogurt, mayonnaise, white wine and mustard. Reserve about 1/3 cup of yogurt mixture. Fold remaining yogurt mixture into chicken or turkey mixture.
2. Spoon about 1/2 cup of chicken or turkey mixture down center of each crepe; roll up. Place, seam-side up, in a 12-inch-square microwave baker. Cover with vented plastic wrap.
3. Microwave at 100% (HIGH) 7 to 8 minutes or until heated through; give dish a half turn after 4 minutes. Place hot crepes on plates. Top each crepe with a dollop of reserved yogurt mixture. Garnish with macadamia nuts and coconut. Makes 4 to 6 servings.

Oven-Fried Chicken

2 tablespoons butter or margarine
1 (3-lb.) broiler-fryer chicken, cut up, without back
1 egg
1 tablespoon water
1 (4.2-oz.) pkg. seasoned crumb-coating chicken

1. Place butter or margarine in a 12" x 7" baking dish. Microwave at 100% (HIGH) 30 seconds or until melted. Set aside.
2. Make a small slit in skin on each piece of chicken. In a pie plate, whisk together egg and water. Dip chicken pieces in egg mixture; then dip in coating mix according to package directions.
3. Place chicken, skin-side down, in butter or margarine with meaty portions toward outside of dish. Microwave at 100% (HIGH) 12 minutes.
4. Turn chicken pieces over. Microwave at 100% (HIGH) 10 minutes. Let stand 5 minutes. Check doneness toward end of cooking time; remove any done pieces. Juices should run clear when chicken is pierced in thickest part. Continue cooking remaining pieces. Makes 3 to 4 servings.

Sherried Chicken Rolls

1/4 cup butter or margarine
1/2 (2-1/2-oz.) jar sliced mushrooms, drained
1/2 cup shredded Swiss cheese (2 oz.)
2 tablespoons chopped parsley
1 teaspoon rubbed sage
6 whole chicken breasts, skinned, boned
2 onions, sliced, separated into rings
1 (10-3/4-oz.) can condensed creamy
    chicken-mushroom soup
1 cup dry sherry

To serve:
Hot cooked rice

1. Place butter or margarine in a 12" x 7" baking dish. Microwave at 100% (HIGH) 1 minute or until melted.
2. In a small bowl, toss together mushrooms, Swiss cheese, parsley and sage. Lay chicken breasts on a flat surface, boned-side up. Spoon mushroom mixture over chicken breasts. Roll up or fold over. Secure with wooden picks. Place in baking dish. Turn chicken pieces over in butter or margarine to coat. Top with sliced onion.
3. In a medium bowl, whisk together soup and sherry. Pour over chicken, coating completely. Cover with vented plastic wrap. Microwave at 100% (HIGH) 10 minutes.
4. Give dish a half turn; rearrange chicken rolls. Microwave at 30% (MEDIUM LOW) 40 minutes or until tender. Let stand, covered, 5 minutes. Place chicken on a serving plate. Stir sauce well; spoon some of sauce over chicken. Serve chicken and sauce with hot cooked rice. Makes 6 servings.

Easy Oven Chicken

1 (3-lb.) broiler-fryer chicken, cut up, without backs
Water or milk to moisten
1 (2-3/8-oz.) envelope seasoned coating mix for chicken

1. Make a small slit in skin on each piece of chicken. Dip chicken pieces in milk or water; drain off excess liquid. Following package directions, shake in coating mix in shaker bag provided.
2. Place chicken, skin-side up, on a microwave rack in a 12" x 7" baking dish. Arrange meaty portions toward outside of dish. Microwave, uncovered, at 100% (HIGH) 19 to 21 minutes. Rearrange chicken pieces once during cooking.
3. Check doneness toward end of cooking time; remove any done pieces. Juices should run clear when chicken is pierced in thickest part. Continue cooking remaining pieces. Makes 3 to 4 servings.

Sherried Chicken Rolls

Roast Broiler-Fryer Chicken

1 recipe Golden Soy Glaze, below
1 (3- to 3-1/4-lb.) whole broiler-fryer chicken

1. Prepare glaze, below. Twist wing tips behind back. Tie legs together tightly with string. Make a small slit in back skin for release of steam. Brush whole chicken with glaze.
2. Place chicken, breast-side down, on a microwave rack in a 12" x 7" baking dish. Cover with a tent of greased waxed paper. Microwave at 100% (HIGH) 10 minutes.
3. Turn chicken breast-side up. Brush with more glaze. Give dish a half turn. Cover with a tent of waxed paper. Microwave at 100% (HIGH) 12 to 14 minutes. Let stand 5 minutes. Juices should run clear when chicken is pierced with a fork between leg and thigh. A microwave meat thermometer inserted between leg and thigh should register 180F (80C).
4. When done, brush chicken with more glaze. Cover tightly with foil; let stand 3 to 5 minutes. Makes 3 to 4 servings.

Variations
Stuffed Broiler-Fryer Chicken: Lightly pack 1-1/4 to 1-1/2 cups stuffing of your choice into body and neck cavities. Skewer openings closed with wooden picks. Microwave as above. Stuffed chicken may need up to 2 minutes longer cooking time. A microwave meat thermometer inserted in center of stuffing must register 165F (75C). If not, continue cooking until this temperature is reached.

Roasting Chicken: A 3-1/2- to 3-3/4-pound roasting chicken without giblets will need about 2 minutes longer microwave cooking time than the unstuffed broiler-fryer chicken. If you want to stuff the chicken, use 2 cups stuffing. Microwave stuffed roasting chicken as above, increasing cooking time to 15 minutes on the first side and to 15 to 20 minutes on the second side. A microwave meat thermometer inserted in center of stuffing must register 165F (75C). If not, continue cooking until this temperature is reached.

Roast Turkey

1 recipe Golden Soy Glaze, below
1 (6- to 8-lb.) frozen whole self-basting turkey, thawed

1. Prepare glaze, below. Remove giblets from turkey. Twist wing tips behind back. Tie legs together tightly with string or replace under band of skin, if present. Make a small slit in back skin for release of steam. Brush whole turkey with glaze.
2. Place turkey, breast-side down, on a microwave rack in a 12" x 7" baking dish. Cover with a tent of greased waxed paper. Microwave at 100% (HIGH) 12 to 15 minutes.
3. Turn turkey breast-side up. Brush with more glaze. Give dish a half turn. Shield wings, ends of drumsticks and top of breast with small pieces of foil if these areas are browning faster than the rest of the bird. Secure foil with wooden picks, if necessary. Cover with a tent of waxed paper.
4. Microwave at 50% (MEDIUM) 65 to 75 minutes; give dish a half turn after 30 minutes. Let stand 5 to 10 minutes. Juices should run clear when turkey is pierced with a fork between leg and thigh. A microwave meat thermometer should register 180F (80C) between leg and thigh and at thickest part of breast meat. When done, brush turkey with more glaze; cover tightly with foil. Let stand 5 minutes. Makes 8 to 10 servings.

Variation
Roast Stuffed Turkey: Lightly pack 2-1/2 to 3 cups stuffing into body cavity and 3/4 to 1-1/4 cups into neck cavity. Skewer openings closed with wooden picks. Microwave as above. A microwave meat thermometer inserted in center of stuffing must register 165F (75C). If not, continue microwaving until this temperature is reached.

Golden Soy Glaze

1 teaspoon cornstarch
2 tablespoons soy sauce
1/3 cup water

1. Combine cornstarch and soy sauce in a small bowl. Stir until blended. Stir in water. Microwave at 100% (HIGH) 1-1/2 to 2 minutes or until thickened; stir every 30 seconds.
2. Brush soy glaze on poultry. Grease waxed paper. Place waxed paper, greased-side down, over glazed poultry, forming a tent. Makes about 1/2 cup.

How to Make Herbed-Chicken Pot Pies

1/Prepare Chicken à la King; stir thawed frozen peas, thyme and sage into hot mixture.

2/Spoon chicken mixture into individual casseroles; heat through. Top each with a pastry round; heat briefly in microwave.

Chicken à la King

1/4 cup butter or margarine
1/4 cup shredded carrot
1/4 cup chopped celery
1/4 cup chopped onion
1/4 cup all-purpose flour
1/2 teaspoon salt
1 cup chicken broth
1 cup half and half
2 cups cubed cooked chicken or turkey
1/2 (2-1/2-oz.) jar sliced mushrooms, drained
1/4 cup chopped pimento
To serve:
Patty shells, toast triangles or mashed potatoes

1. In a deep 2-quart casserole, combine butter or margarine, carrot, celery and onion. Microwave at 100% (HIGH) 5 minutes or until vegetables are tender; stir after 2-1/2 minutes.
2. Blend in flour and salt. Microwave at 100% (HIGH) 30 seconds. Stir in broth and half and half. Microwave at 100% (HIGH) 4 to 5 minutes or until thickened and bubbly; stir every minute. Mixture should be thick and smooth.
3. Stir in chicken or turkey, mushrooms and pimento; cover. Microwave at 100% (HIGH) 3 minutes or until heated through. Stir; serve in patty shells, or over toast triangles or mashed potatoes. Makes 4 servings.

Herbed-Chicken Pot Pies

2 sticks pie-crust mix
1 cup frozen green peas, thawed
1/2 teaspoon dried leaf thyme
1/2 teaspoon dried rubbed sage
4 cups hot Chicken à la King, at left

1. Prepare pie-crust mix according to package directions. On a lightly floured board, roll out pastry to 1/8 inch thick. Cut in 4 circles 1 inch larger than tops of 4 individual casseroles. Fold under edges of pastry; flute so pastry will fit inside tops of casseroles. Pierce pastry with a fork or use a cookie cutter to make a chicken-shape cutout in center of each round.
2. Place pastry rounds on a 12-inch platter. Microwave at 70% (MEDIUM HIGH) 7-1/2 to 8 minutes or until barely done; give platter a half turn after 4 minutes. Cool pastry rounds on a wire rack.
3. Stir peas, thyme and sage into hot Chicken à la King. Spoon hot chicken mixture into individual casseroles. Cover with vented plastic wrap. Microwave at 100% (HIGH) 6 to 7 minutes or until heated through, rearranging once.
4. Uncover casseroles; stir fillings. Top each casserole with a pastry round. Microwave, uncovered, at 100% (HIGH) 2 minutes or until pastry is warm. Makes 4 servings.

Fish & Seafood

Use the microwave oven to produce delicious summer dishes without heating up your kitchen.

Q. How is fish cooked in the microwave?

A. Because fish is already tender, most varieties cook very satisfactorily at 100% (HIGH) in the microwave.

Q. What are the disadvantages of cooking fish in the microwave?

A. Shellfish becomes tough if overcooked in the microwave. Watch shellfish carefully and test for doneness before the end of the cooking time.

Q. Can fish be pan-fried in the microwave?

A. Breaded fish can be cooked quickly and successfully in the microwave with special browning skillets. The opposite is true for batter-coated fish which tends to get soggy when cooked in the browning skillet. Frozen fish portions and fish sticks that are breaded give particularly good results.

Purchasing Fish & Shellfish

Fish and shellfish are extremely perishable. Purchase them the day they are to be eaten if possible. Fresh fish should have a mild aroma. The *fishy* smell develops with age. Flesh should be firm and spring back when pressed. Check packages of frozen fish and shellfish for signs of damage and thawing. Keep frozen until needed. For many recipes, fish can be cooked frozen or partially thawed.

Q. Which fish or seafood dishes do not cook satisfactorily in the microwave?

A. Fish cannot be deep-fried in the microwave. Whole live lobsters require a large kettle of boiling water and this takes too long in the microwave. And, a kettle holding enough water for more than one or two lobsters is too large for this appliance.

Q. How do you know when fish is done?

A. Using the tines of a fork, gently lift up the flesh in the center of the fish. The flesh should be beginning to flake. It will continue cooking during the standing time. Shellfish usually turns from translucent in its raw state to opaque when cooked.

Q. Can fish be reheated in the microwave?

A. This is not recommended unless the fish is heated in a sauce. Fish overcooks quickly. The reheating time is often equal to the original cooking time and the fish will become tough from overcooking.

Q. How do you defrost fish in the microwave?

A. Fish is easy to defrost in the microwave. Start with a 30% (MEDIUM LOW) defrosting time, then a 10% (LOW) defrosting time, plus standing time in cold water.

Q. Are any special utensils needed to cook fish in the microwave?

A. If you often cook whole fish, a large microwave fish-baking dish can be very useful. It's difficult to find other baking dishes big enough to accommodate a large whole fish.

Creamy Stuffed Manicotti, page 38

Creamy Scalloped Oysters

1/2 cup butter or margarine
2 cups oyster crackers, crushed
2 tablespoons chopped parsley
1 tablespoon chopped chives
1/4 teaspoon paprika
1 pint shucked oysters
3/4 cup whipping cream
1/4 teaspoon hot-pepper sauce
1/4 teaspoon freshly ground pepper

1. Place butter or margarine in a 1-1/2-quart bowl. Micro-wave at 100% (HIGH) 1-3/4 minutes or until melted. Stir cracker crumbs, parsley, chives and paprika into melted butter or margarine. Reserve 1/3 of cracker mixture for topping.
2. Drain oysters, reserving 2 tablespoons liquor. Add oysters to remaining cracker mixture. In a small bowl, combine oyster liquor, whipping cream, hot-pepper sauce and pepper. Mix well. Stir into oyster mixture.
3. Spoon into a 8-inch-round baking dish. Cover with vented plastic wrap. Microwave at 50% (MEDIUM) 9 to 10 minutes or until heated through; stir every 3 minutes. Stir again and top with reserved crumb mixture. Microwave, uncovered, at 50% (MEDIUM) 1 minute or until crumbs are heated through. Makes 4 servings.

Cooking Fish

Cook fish until it begins to flake when a fork is inserted into the thickest part. Another guide is to cook fish until it turns from translucent to opaque. Fish will continue to cook during the standing time. *Caution:* Overcooked fish is tough and dry.

Creamy Stuffed Manicotti

Zucchini Sauce:
1/4 cup butter or margarine
2 cups coarsely chopped zucchini
1/2 cup sliced green onion
1/2 cup chopped pimento
1/4 cup all-purpose flour
1 teaspoon celery salt
1/4 teaspoon pepper
1-3/4 cups milk

Filling:
1 egg
1 cup (8 oz.) cream-style cottage cheese
1 (9-1/4-oz.) can water-pack tuna, drained, flaked
1/2 cup herb-seasoned stuffing mix
1/2 cup chopped ripe olives
1/4 cup grated Parmesan cheese
2 tablespoons chopped parsley
1 teaspoon chopped chives
8 manicotti shells, cooked, drained

To garnish:
Snipped chives

---

1. To make sauce, in a 1-1/2-quart casserole, combine butter or margarine, zucchini and green onion. Microwave at 100% (HIGH) 3 to 5 minutes or until barely tender. Stir in pimento. Blend in flour, celery salt and pepper.
2. Microwave at 100% (HIGH) 30 seconds. Whisk in milk. Microwave at 100% (HIGH) 5 to 7 minutes or until mixture thickens and bubbles; stir every 2 minutes. Mixture should be thick and smooth.
3. Pour 1/2 of sauce into a 12" x 7" baking dish. Set aside remaining sauce.
4. To make filling, beat egg in a medium bowl. Stir in cottage cheese, tuna, stuffing mix, olives, Parmesan cheese, parsley and chives. Mix well. Spoon about 1/2 cup cottage-cheese mixture into each manicotti shell. Place stuffed manicotti on top of sauce in baking dish.
5. Pour remaining sauce over manicotti, coating all pasta. Cover with vented plastic wrap. Microwave at 50% (MEDIUM) 20 to 25 minutes or until heated through, giving dish a half turn once. At the end of cooking time, stir sauce and spoon over manicotti shells. Let stand, covered, 5 minutes. Garnish with additional chopped chives. Makes 4 to 6 servings.

How to Make Easy Herbed-Halibut Steaks

1/Arrange halibut steaks with thickest portions toward outside of baking dish; spread with cheese mixture.

2/Serve herbed-halibut steaks with buttered green beans, canned spiced peaches and hot blueberry muffins.

Easy Herbed-Halibut Steaks

1/2 (4-oz.) carton semi-soft natural cheese with garlic and herbs
1/4 cup Tangy Tartar Sauce, at right, or prepared tartar sauce
4 (6-oz.) halibut steaks, 3/4 inch thick
12 cucumber slices
1/2 cup shredded Cheddar cheese (2 oz.)
1 tablespoon chopped chives

1. In a small bowl, whisk together semi-soft cheese and tartar sauce. Arrange halibut steaks in a 12" x 7" baking dish, placing larger pieces and thicker portions toward outside of dish. Spread steaks with cheese mixture.
2. Cover with vented plastic wrap. Microwave at 100% (HIGH) 7 to 8 minutes or until center of fish is beginning to flake when tested with a fork. Give dish a half turn after 4 minutes.
3. Top steaks with cucumber slices. Sprinkle with Cheddar cheese and chopped chives. Microwave, uncovered, at 100% (HIGH) 2-1/2 minutes or until cheese melts. Let stand, covered, 5 minutes. Makes 4 servings.

Tangy Tartar Sauce

1/4 cup plain yogurt
1/4 cup mayonnaise or salad dressing
1/4 cup chopped dill pickle
1/4 cup sliced pimento-stuffed green olives
1/8 teaspoon onion powder
1/8 teaspoon freshly ground pepper

1. In a medium bowl, combine all ingredients. Mix well.
2. Cover and refrigerate until serving time. Serve with hot or cold fish dishes. Makes about 1 cup.

Hearty Fish Stew

2 tablespoons butter or margarine
1/2 cup cubed peeled rutabaga
1/4 cup chopped onion
1-1/2 cups fish stock or chicken broth
2 tomatoes, peeled, quartered
2 ears corn-on-the-cob, cut in 1-1/2-inch pieces
1/2 teaspoon dried leaf basil
1/2 teaspoon dried leaf oregano
1/2 teaspoon salt
1 lb. fish fillets or steaks, poached, chilled
1 medium zucchini, cut in 1-inch pieces

1. In a deep 2-quart casserole with lid, combine butter or margarine, rutabaga and onion. Cover. Microwave at 100% (HIGH) 5 minutes or until onion is tender.
2. Stir in fish stock or chicken broth, tomatoes, corn, basil, oregano and salt. Cover. Microwave at 100% (HIGH) 18 to 20 minutes or until vegetables are barely tender; stir after 9 minutes.
3. Break fish into chunks. Add fish to casserole with zucchini. Cover. Microwave at 100% (HIGH) 3 to 4 minutes or until fish is heated through and zucchini is crisp-tender. Makes 3 to 4 servings.

Luncheon Seashells

1 tablespoon butter or margarine
3 tablespoons dry bread crumbs
3 tablespoons grated Parmesan cheese
1 tablespoon chopped parsley
3 tablespoons butter or margarine
3 tablespoons all-purpose flour
1/2 teaspoon dried leaf thyme
1/4 teaspoon celery salt
1/8 teaspoon pepper
1 cup fish stock or chicken broth
1/2 cup half and half
1 lb. fish or scallops, poached, cubed (2-1/4 cups cubed)
1 (14-oz.) can artichoke hearts, drained, quartered
1 (2-1/2-oz.) jar sliced mushrooms, drained

1. Place 1 tablespoon butter or margarine in a 2-cup bowl. Microwave at 100% (HIGH) 30 seconds or until melted. Stir in bread crumbs, Parmesan cheese and parsley; set aside.
2. Place 3 tablespoons butter or margarine in a 1-quart glass measuring cup. Microwave at 100% (HIGH) 1 minute or until melted. Stir in flour, thyme, celery salt and pepper.
3. Microwave at 100% (HIGH) 30 seconds. Stir in fish stock or chicken broth and half and half. Microwave at 100% (HIGH) 3 to 4 minutes or until thickened and bubbly; stir every minute. Mixture should be thick and smooth.
4. Fold in fish or scallops, artichoke hearts and mushrooms. Spoon into 4 (5-1/2-inch) baking shells or individual casseroles. Microwave at 100% (HIGH) 6 to 8 minutes or until heated through; rearrange shells after 3 minutes. Sprinkle with crumb mixture. Makes 4 servings.

Shrimp Creole

2 bacon slices, diced
1/3 cup chopped celery
1/3 cup chopped onion
1 large garlic clove, minced
1 (28-oz.) can tomatoes
1 cup chili sauce
1-1/2 teaspoons dried leaf thyme
1/4 teaspoon salt
1/4 teaspoon pepper
1/4 teaspoon hot-pepper sauce
3-1/2 cups cooked peeled shrimp

To serve:
Hot cooked rice

1. In a deep 3-quart casserole, combine bacon, celery, onion and garlic. Microwave at 100% (HIGH) 5 minutes or until vegetables are tender; stir after 2 minutes. Chop tomatoes, reserving juice. Stir in chopped tomatoes with juice, chili sauce, thyme, salt, pepper and hot-pepper sauce. Mix well. Cover.
2. Microwave at 100% (HIGH) 6 minutes or until boiling. Stir. Cover. Microwave at 30% (MEDIUM LOW) 20 minutes. Stir in shrimp. Cover. Microwave at 100% (HIGH) 4 to 5 minutes or until heated through; stir after 2 minutes. Serve over hot cooked rice. Makes 6 servings.

Pan-Fried Fish Fillets

1/4 cup milk
1/4 cup yellow cornmeal
1/4 cup packaged biscuit mix
1/4 cup all-purpose flour
1 tablespoon sesame seeds
1/2 teaspoon paprika
1/2 teaspoon celery salt
1/8 teaspoon onion powder
1 lb. fish fillets, 1/4 to 1/2 inch thick
1/4 cup vegetable oil

1. Pour milk into a pie plate. In another pie plate, mix together cornmeal, biscuit mix, flour, sesame seeds, paprika, celery salt and onion powder. Dip fish fillets in milk to moisten both sides; drain off excess milk. Dip in cornmeal mixture; coat both sides. Place breaded fish on a rack; set aside.
2. Preheat a 10-inch microwave browning skillet at 100% (HIGH) 4 minutes. Add oil to skillet. Using hot pads, tilt skillet so entire surface is coated with oil. Quickly add fish. If fillets have skin, place skin-side up. Microwave on first side at 100% (HIGH) 1-1/2 minutes.
3. Turn fish over and give dish a half turn. Microwave at 100% (HIGH) 1-1/2 to 2 minutes or until browned and center of fish is beginning to flake when tested with a fork. Makes 3 or 4 servings.

Variation
Pan-Fried Filleted Trout: Tie whole trout together with string. Use milk and breading mixture as above. Preheat browning skillet 4 minutes. Add 1/4 cup oil as above. Microwave 2 (8-ounce) trout at 100% (HIGH) 2 minutes. Turn trout over. Microwave at 100% (HIGH) 2 minutes or until center of fish is beginning to flake when tested with a fork.

How to Make Fish in a Clay Pot

1/Chop leeks, radishes and fennel to use as a stuffing mixture. This two-level cutting board makes chopping easier.

2/Spoon vegetable stuffing into fish cavity. It may be necessary to remove head and tail so fish will fit clay pot.

3/Tie fish cavity closed with string. Soak sorrel or spinach leaves in hot water to make them pliable and easy to wind around fish.

4/Place stuffed fish on a microwave rack or inverted saucers in clay pot; drizzle with wine and butter sauce.

Fish in a Clay Pot

Sorrel or spinach leaves
1 (3- to 3-1/2-lb.) cleaned whole fish
Garlic salt to taste
1/4 cup chopped fennel
1/4 cup chopped leeks
1/4 cup chopped radishes
3 tablespoons butter or margarine
3 tablespoons dry white wine

1. Soak a 4-quart clay pot and lid in cold water 20 minutes or according to manufacturer's directions. Soak sorrel or spinach leaves in hot water. Sprinkle cavity of fish with garlic salt.
2. In a small bowl, combine fennel, leeks and radishes. Stuff vegetable mixture into fish cavity. Tie fish cavity with string to hold in stuffing. Drain sorrel or spinach. Wrap sorrel or spinach leaves around entire fish.
3. Place fish on a microwave rack or inverted saucers in soaked clay pot. Place butter or margarine in a glass baking cup. Microwave at 100% (HIGH) 45 to 60 seconds or until melted. Stir in wine. Drizzle butter or margarine mixture over fish. Cover with clay-pot lid.
4. Microwave at 100% (HIGH) 40 to 45 minutes or until center of fish is beginning to flake when tested with a fork. Give clay pot a half turn after 20 minutes. Serve fish with cooking juices. Makes 6 servings.

Eggs & Cheese

Q. How are eggs cooked in the microwave?

A. Because eggs are already tender, most egg dishes cook well at 100% (HIGH). The exceptions are quiches and layered casseroles. They are cooked at a lower power so the centers will get done without overcooking the edges.

Q. Which egg dishes do not cook satisfactorily in the microwave?

A. Never try to cook an egg in the shell in the microwave. The egg will explode, making a considerable mess in the oven. To cook whole eggs out of the shell, prick the yolk with a fork or wooden pick. The yolk has a high fat content and consequently attracts microwaves more than the white. In addition, the yolk has an outer membrane that has the same effect as the egg shell, so unpricked yolks are likely to explode. Egg dishes that rely on the puffiness of beaten egg whites are not successful in the microwave. Soufflés or puffy omelets puff beautifully while they are being cooked in the microwave, but they fall immediately when removed. Even using low power levels, the outside edges will be tough and overcooked by the time the center of the soufflé is done.

Q. How do you know when eggs are done?

A. For most egg dishes in large casseroles, a knife inserted in the center should feel hot. Cooking casseroles is deceiving; the edges will bubble vigorously before the center is even warm. That is why bringing the edges of the casserole to the center promotes more even heating.

Q. Can egg and cheese dishes be reheated in the microwave?

A. Wedges of quiche and servings of casseroles reheat well in the microwave. Other items such as scrambled eggs cook so quickly in the microwave, it's best to start over. Reheating eggs tends to overcook and toughen them.

Q. What about cooking convenience egg and cheese dishes?

A. Many frozen TV breakfasts and cheese casseroles have microwave cooking directions on the package.

Q. Are any special utensils needed to cook eggs in the microwave?

A. Browning skillets are necessary to fry eggs in the microwave. For quiches you can use the same ceramic or glass quiche dishes or pie plates that you use in a conventional oven.

Microwave Cautions

Never microwave a whole egg in the shell. The egg will explode into more pieces than you can imagine. Not only does this make a tremendous mess inside your microwave oven, it can be dangerous if the egg explodes in your face.

Never reheat a whole hard-cooked egg in the microwave. Some hard-cooked eggs may explode if they are reheated whole. Always slice or quarter hard-cooked eggs before reheating.

Never poach, bake or fry an egg in the microwave without pricking the yolk. The egg yolk is covered by a thin membrane. If this membrane is not pricked before microwaving, the yolk may explode.

Chicken Quiche, page 48

Sunshine Omelet Filling

2 teaspoons butter or margarine
1/2 cup chopped zucchini
2 tablespoons shredded carrot
2 tablespoons chopped green onion
1/4 teaspoon dried leaf basil
6 cherry tomatoes, halved
2 teaspoons sunflower kernels

1. In a 1-quart casserole, combine butter or margarine, zucchini, carrot, green onion and basil. Microwave, uncovered, at 100% (HIGH) 2-1/2 to 3 minutes or until vegetables are tender; stir once. Add tomatoes.
2. Microwave at 100% (HIGH) 45 to 60 seconds or until heated through. Stir in sunflower kernels. Use mixture as filling for French Omelet, opposite, or other omelet. Makes 2/3 cup.

Scrambled Eggs

4 eggs
1/4 cup milk
Dash salt
Dash pepper
2 teaspoons butter or margarine, cut in pieces

1. In a deep 1-quart bowl, whisk together eggs, milk, salt and pepper. Dot with butter or margarine. Cover with vented plastic wrap. Microwave at 70% (MEDIUM HIGH) 2-1/2 minutes or until about half set; stir.
2. Microwave at 70% (MEDIUM HIGH) 1-1/4 to 1-1/2 minutes or until almost set. Stir. Let stand, covered, 1 minute before serving. Makes 2 servings.

Bacon & Eggs

2 bacon slices, halved
2 eggs

1. Preheat a 10-inch microwave browning skillet at 100% (HIGH) 3 minutes. Quickly add bacon to 1 end of skillet. Microwave, uncovered, at 100% (HIGH) 30 to 60 seconds.
2. Turn bacon over. Using hot pads, tilt skillet to coat with drippings. Break eggs into a cup. Gently add eggs to other end of skillet. Prick yolks with a fork or wooden pick. Microwave, uncovered, at 100% (HIGH) 1-1/2 to 2 minutes or until eggs are done as desired. Let stand, covered, 1 minute. Makes 2 servings.

Scrambled Eggs Deluxe

6 tablespoons butter or margarine
3 cups sliced fresh mushrooms
1/3 cup chopped green onions
1 medium garlic clove, minced
1 (14-oz.) can artichoke hearts, drained, halved
6 eggs, beaten
1-1/2 cups shredded Cheddar cheese (6 oz.)
2-1/2 cups cubed cooked ham (13 oz.)
1/3 cup seasoned dry bread crumbs
1 (3-oz.) can French-fried onions

1. In a 12" x 7" baking dish, combine butter or margarine, mushrooms, green onions and garlic. Cover with vented plastic wrap. Microwave at 100% (HIGH) 5 to 6 minutes or until onions are tender; stir after 3 minutes.
2. Stir in artichoke hearts, eggs, cheese, ham and bread crumbs. Mix well. Cover with vented plastic wrap. Microwave at 70% (MEDIUM HIGH) 12 to 14 minutes or until eggs are almost set; stir after 6 minutes.
3. Top with French-fried onions. Microwave, uncovered, at 100% (HIGH) 2 minutes or until onions are warm; serve immediately. Makes 6 servings.

How to Make French Omelet

1/Pour beaten egg mixture into melted butter in a pie plate. Cover pie plate completely with plastic wrap. Do not vent plastic wrap or portions of omelet will not cook. Microwave at 70% 1-1/2 minutes.

2/Gently lift cooked edges; let uncooked egg flow underneath. Cover with unvented plastic wrap; continue microwaving. Fill with Sunshine Omelet Filling, opposite, or Bacon Omelet Filling, below.

French Omelet

2/3 cup Bacon Omelet Filling, at right, or
    Sunshine Omelet Filling, opposite
1 tablespoon butter or margarine
3 eggs
3 tablespoons milk
Dash salt
Dash pepper

1. Prepare filling for omelet; set aside. Place butter or margarine in a 9-inch pie plate. Microwave at 100% (HIGH) 30 seconds or until melted.
2. Beat together eggs, milk, salt and pepper. Add to pie plate. Cover completely with plastic wrap; do not vent. Microwave at 70% (MEDIUM HIGH) 1-1/2 minutes.
3. Remove wrap. Gently lift cooked egg edges, allowing uncooked egg to flow underneath. Cover completely with unvented plastic wrap. Microwave at 70% (MEDIUM HIGH) 1-1/2 to 1-3/4 minutes or until almost set. Let stand, covered, 1 minute.
4. Fill with prepared filling. Fold over; serve immediately. Makes 2 servings.

Bacon Omelet Filling

4 bacon slices
4 thin onion slices, separated in rings
4 green-bell-pepper rings
1/2 teaspoon dried leaf Italian herbs

1. Place bacon on a microwave rack in a 12" x 7" baking dish. Cover with a white paper towel. Microwave at 100% (HIGH) 3-1/2 to 4 minutes or until crisp. Drain bacon on paper towels, reserving pan drippings. Crumble bacon; set aside.
2. Remove microwave rack. Discard all but 4 teaspoons bacon drippings. Stir in onion, green-pepper rings and Italian herbs. Microwave, uncovered, at 100% (HIGH) 3-1/2 to 4-1/2 minutes or until tender; stir once. Drain off excess drippings.
3. Stir in crumbled bacon. Use mixture as filling for French Omelet, at left, or other omelet. Makes 2/3 cup.

Overnight Brunch Casserole

2 tablespoons butter or margarine
2 tablespoons all-purpose flour
1-1/4 cups milk
1 (4-oz.) carton semi-soft natural cheese with garlic and
  herbs
8 oz. bulk pork sausage
1/4 cup chopped green onions
1/4 cup chopped pimento-stuffed green olives
1 cup drained cooked whole-kernel corn or green peas
12 eggs, beaten

To garnish:
Tomato wedges
Chopped parsley

1. Place butter or margarine in a 1-quart glass measuring
cup. Microwave at 100% (HIGH) 45 seconds or until
melted. Stir in flour. Microwave at 100% (HIGH) 30
seconds. Whisk in milk. Microwave at 100% (HIGH) 2-1/2
to 3 minutes or until mixture thickens and bubbles; stir
every minute. Mixture should be thick and smooth. Stir in
cheese. Microwave at 100% (HIGH) 1 minute or until
cheese melts. Stir until smooth; set aside.
2. In a 12" x 7" baking dish, combine sausage and green
onions. Microwave at 100% (HIGH) 5 minutes or until
sausage is browned and done; stir every 2 minutes. Drain
well.
3. Stir in olives, corn or peas and eggs. Cover with vented
plastic wrap. Microwave at 70% (MEDIUM HIGH) 8 minutes or until eggs are almost set; stir every 3 minutes. Fold
in cheese sauce.
4. Cover with plastic wrap; refrigerate overnight. To
serve, vent plastic wrap. Microwave at 70% (MEDIUM
HIGH) 8 to 10 minutes or until heated through; stir twice.
Top with tomato wedges. Microwave at 70% (MEDIUM
HIGH) 2 to 3 minutes or until tomatoes are warmed. Sprinkle with parsley. Makes 8 servings.

Chicken Quiche

2 cups shredded Gruyère cheese (8 oz.)
1 (10-inch) baked, unpricked pastry shell
1 tablespoon butter or margarine, room temperature
1 cup cubed cooked chicken
1/4 cup chopped green onion
1/3 cup cooked drained whole-kernel corn
1 pint half and half (2 cups)
1/4 teaspoon salt
1/2 teaspoon rubbed sage
1/2 teaspoon dried leaf thyme
5 eggs, beaten

1. Sprinkle shredded cheese into baked pastry shell.
2. In a 1-quart casserole, combine butter or margarine,
chicken, green onion and corn. Cover with waxed paper.
Microwave at 100% (HIGH) 2 to 3 minutes or until onion
is tender. Drain very well. Add well-drained filling to
pastry shell; set aside.
3. In a 1-quart glass measuring cup, combine half and half,
salt, sage and thyme. Microwave at 100% (HIGH) 2-1/2 to
3-1/2 minutes or until almost boiling.
4. Gradually stir half-and-half mixture into eggs. Pour into
pastry shell. Microwave, uncovered, at 50% (MEDIUM) 17
to 19 minutes or until a knife inserted off-center comes
out clean. Give quiche a quarter turn every 9 minutes.
Center should jiggle slightly. Let stand 10 minutes. Knife
inserted just off center should come out clean. Quiche will
set upon standing. Makes 8 servings.

Cooking Cheese

Because most cheeses are high in fat, they attract
the microwaves. This causes cheese to melt quickly. If
cheese is used as a topping, add it towards the end of
the cooking time. Cheese stirred into a casserole cooks
more slowly because it is mixed with other
ingredients. Overcooked cheese is tough and stringy.

Old-Fashioned Cheese Rarebit

3/4 cup half and half
1/2 cup shredded process American cheese (2 oz.)
1/2 cup shredded process Swiss cheese (2 oz.)
1 tablespoon all-purpose flour
1/2 teaspoon dry mustard
1 teaspoon Worcestershire sauce
1 egg yolk, beaten

1. Pour half and half into a 1-quart bowl. Microwave at 100% (HIGH) 1-1/2 to 2 minutes or until almost boiling. In a small bowl, toss together cheeses, flour and dry mustard. Gradually add cheese mixture to hot half and half, whisking well after each addition. Whisk in Worcestershire sauce.
2. Microwave at 100% (HIGH) 1 to 1-1/2 minutes or until cheeses are melted; stir 3 times. Whisk until smooth. Gradually stir half the hot sauce into egg yolk; mix well. Stir yolk mixture into remaining hot sauce in bowl.
3. Microwave at 100% (HIGH) 45 to 60 seconds or until thickened and heated through; stir every 15 seconds. Serve over toasted English muffins or open-face sandwiches. Makes 2 servings.

Smoky Eggs à la King

2 tablespoons butter or margarine
1/2 cup chopped zucchini
3 tablespoons chopped onion
2 tablespoons all-purpose flour
1/2 cup milk
1/2 cup chicken broth
1/2 (2-1/2-oz.) pkg. sliced smoked beef, snipped
2 hard-cooked eggs, sliced
2 tablespoons chopped pimento

To serve:
Chow mein noodles, warmed

1. In a deep 1-quart casserole, combine butter or margarine, zucchini and onion. Microwave at 100% (HIGH) 3 minutes or until vegetables are tender; stir once. Stir in flour; mix well. Microwave at 100% (HIGH) 30 seconds or until bubbly.
2. Whisk in milk and broth. Microwave at 100% (HIGH) 2-1/2 to 3-1/2 minutes or until thickened and bubbly; stir every minute. Mixture should be thick and smooth.
3. Stir in beef, eggs and pimento. Cover. Microwave at 100% (HIGH) 2 to 2-1/2 minutes or until heated through; stir after 1 minute. Stir; serve over chow mein noodles. Makes 3 to 4 servings.

Cheese-Lover's Lasagna

1 egg
2 tablespoons all-purpose flour
1 cup cream-style cottage cheese
1/2 cup grated Parmesan cheese (1-1/2 oz.)
1/4 cup shredded carrot
1/4 cup chopped celery
1/4 cup chopped pimento
1/4 cup chopped green onions
1 (10-oz.) pkg. frozen chopped spinach, cooked, drained well
2 tablespoons all-purpose flour
1/2 cup plain yogurt
1 (10-3/4-oz.) can condensed cream of onion soup
6 plain or whole-wheat lasagna noodles, cooked, drained well
8 oz. sliced sharp process American cheese

1. Butter a 12" x 7" baking dish; set aside. In a medium bowl, beat egg. Stir in 2 tablespoons flour, cottage cheese and Parmesan cheese. Fold carrot, celery, pimento, green onions and spinach into cottage-cheese filling; set aside.
2. In a medium bowl, whisk 2 tablespoons flour into yogurt. Whisk in soup, mixing well. In buttered baking dish, layer 1/2 of noodles, then 1/2 each of the cottage-cheese mixture, process cheese and yogurt sauce. Repeat layers.
3. Cover with vented plastic wrap. Microwave at 50% (MEDIUM) 25 to 30 minutes or until hot in center, giving dish a half turn once. Let stand, uncovered, 10 minutes. Makes 6 servings.

Mushroom-Macaroni Bake

2 tablespoons butter or margarine
2 cups sliced fresh mushrooms
1/2 cup chopped red or green bell pepper
1/4 cup chopped onion
1 (10-3/4-oz.) can condensed cream of onion soup
3/4 cup milk
1/2 teaspoon dried dill weed
2 cups shredded Edam cheese (8 oz.)
2 cups medium-shell macaroni (7 oz.), cooked, drained
1 (9-oz.) pkg. frozen Italian green beans, cooked, drained

To garnish:
Sunflower kernels, if desired
Chopped parsley, if desired

1. In a deep 2-quart casserole, combine butter or margarine, mushrooms, red or green pepper and onion. Cover. Microwave at 100% (HIGH) 4 to 5 minutes or until vegetables are just tender; stir once.
2. Stir in soup, milk and dill weed. Mix well. Stir in cheese, macaroni and green beans. Cover. Microwave at 100% (HIGH) 10 to 12 minutes or until heated through; stir once. Stir before serving.
3. Garnish with sunflower kernels and parsley, if desired. Makes 5 to 6 servings.

How to Make Cheese-Lover's Lasagna

1/Press cooked spinach in a sieve to remove excess moisture. Spinach must be well-drained or filling will be watery.

2/Shredded carrot, chopped celery, pimento, green onion and spinach are folded into cottage-cheese filling.

3/Whisk flour into yogurt. Whisk in onion soup. Flour helps keep yogurt from curdling.

4/Layer 1/2 of lasagna noodles; then 1/2 each of cottage-cheese filling, cheese slices and yogurt sauce. Repeat layers. Microwave lasagna until hot.

Shirred Eggs

4 teaspoons butter or margarine
4 eggs
Dash seasoned salt
1/4 cup shredded Cheddar cheese (1 oz.)

To garnish:
Chopped parsley

1. Butter 4 (6-ounce) glass baking cups. Place 1 teaspoon butter or margarine in bottom of each cup. Microwave at 100% (HIGH) 20 seconds or until melted.
2. Gently slip 1 egg into each cup. Prick yolks with a fork or wooden pick. Sprinkle with seasoned salt and cheese. Cover each cup with vented plastic wrap. Microwave at 70% (MEDIUM HIGH) 3 to 3-1/2 minutes or until eggs are just set; rearrange cups after 1 minute. Give them a half turn after 2 minutes. Let stand, covered, 1 minute. Sprinkle with parsley. Makes 4 servings.

Vegetables & Salads

Q. What are the advantages of cooking vegetables in the microwave?

A. Vegetables have more flavor when cooked in the microwave because they cook more quickly. They usually require little or no water that might dilute some of the flavor. Studies indicate that vegetables cooked in the microwave actually retain more vitamins and minerals.

Q. Which vegetable dishes do not cook satisfactorily in the microwave?

A. Vegetable soufflés do not work in the microwave because the egg structure cannot be set without overcooking the edges of the soufflé. Commercially frozen vegetable soufflés can be reheated in the microwave because the structure is already set.

Q. How are vegetables cooked in the microwave?

A. Most fresh, frozen and canned vegetables are cooked at 100% (HIGH). Many fresh vegetables have directions for a unique method of cooking. They are blanched, or partially cooked, and then refrigerated. Shortly before serving time, the vegetables are reheated with butter in the microwave. This is an easy make-ahead method to use for entertaining. Vegetables frozen in pouches are microwaved right in the pouch after a small slit is cut on one side of the pouch. It's handy to blanch and freeze your own vegetables in family-size pouches. If you have a small family, buy frozen loose-pack vegetables in large plastic bags. Follow directions in this chapter to cook the amount you need.

Q. How do you know when vegetables are done?

A. The cooking times given are for crisp-tender vegetables. When pierced with a fork, crisp-tender vegetables will still have a little resistance. Vegetables continue to cook during the standing time, so allow for that when estimating doneness. If you prefer well-done vegetables, add cooking time in 30- to 60-second amounts. Baked potatoes should be cooked until still slightly firm, then wrapped in foil for the standing time to finish cooking. Potatoes cooked until tender to the touch will be shriveled by the time they are served.

Q. Can vegetable convenience foods be cooked in the microwave?

A. Yes. Many frozen vegetable casseroles or combinations with sauces have microwave directions on the package. Many of the dry packaged vegetables, such as potatoes, also have microwave cooking directions on the package.

Q. Why do you stir or rearrange vegetables during cooking?

A. Vegetables are stirred during cooking so they will cook more evenly. If they are not moved around, the vegetables close to the edges of the dish will overcook before the vegetables in the center are done. To rearrange vegetables in a pouch, pick up the pouch and flex it several times to move the frozen vegetables in the center toward the outside of the pouch. In the case of larger vegetables that cannot be stirred, move the center pieces to the outside of the dish and the pieces from the outside to the center.

Q. Why are vegetables salted after cooking?

A. Unless the salt is dissolved in a sauce, vegetables should be salted after cooking. Otherwise, salt lying on the surface of the vegetables may cause dehydration and shriveling where it touches the vegetables.

Garnish cooked vegetables with crumbled bacon, flavored croutons, toasted nuts or shredded cheese.

Confetti Asparagus Bake, page 54

Blanched & Butter-Cooked Asparagus

1-1/4 lb. fresh asparagus spears
1/4 cup water
2 tablespoons butter or margarine

1. Wash asparagus. Grasp stalk at either end and bend in a bow shape. Stalk will break where tender part of stalk starts. Discard tough part of stalk.
2. Place spears in a 2- to 3-quart casserole with lid. Add water. Cover. Microwave at 100% (HIGH) 6 minutes or until crisp-tender; rearrange spears after 3 minutes. Drain in a colander; run cold water over asparagus. Wrap and refrigerate.
3. At serving time, melt butter or margarine in clean casserole at 100% (HIGH) 30 seconds. Add asparagus, stirring to coat. Cover. Microwave at 100% (HIGH) 4 to 5 minutes or until heated through; stir once. Let stand, covered, 2 minutes. Makes 4 to 5 servings.

Confetti Asparagus Bake

2 (10-oz.) pkgs. frozen asparagus spears
1/4 cup butter or margarine
2 tablespoons seasoned dry bread crumbs
3 tablespoons finely chopped onion
3 tablespoons finely chopped celery
1 tomato, chopped, drained
1/4 teaspoon dried leaf basil, crushed
1/4 teaspoon dried leaf thyme, crushed
2 tablespoons grated Parmesan cheese

1. Loosen wrapping on asparagus packages. Place packages in microwave oven on paper towels. Microwave at 100% (HIGH) 3 minutes. On a round 12-inch microwave platter, arrange asparagus spears, spoke-fashion, with tips pointing to center.
2. In a small bowl, microwave butter or margarine at 100% (HIGH) 1 minute or until melted. Combine 1 tablespoon melted butter or margarine with bread crumbs; set aside.
3. Sprinkle onion, celery and tomato pieces over asparagus; drizzle with remaining melted butter or margarine. Sprinkle with basil and thyme. Cover with vented plastic wrap. Microwave at 100% (HIGH) 10 to 11 minutes or until asparagus is tender, giving platter a half turn after 5 minutes. Sprinkle with Parmesan cheese and buttered crumbs. Makes 6 servings.

Blanched & Butter-Cooked Broccoli

1 lb. fresh broccoli
1/4 cup water
1 tablespoon butter or margarine

1. Wash broccoli; cut into flowerets, leaving 1 to 2 inches of stalk. Place in a 1-quart casserole with lid, with stems toward outside of dish. Add water. Cover. Microwave at 100% (HIGH) 6 to 7 minutes or until starting to get tender.
2. Drain in a colander; rinse under running water. Wrap and refrigerate. At serving time, melt butter or margarine in clean casserole at 100% (HIGH) 45 seconds. Add broccoli; stir to coat. Cover. Microwave at 100% (HIGH) 4 to 5 minutes or until tender and heated through; stir once. Let stand, covered, 2 minutes. Makes 4 servings.

How to Make Zesty Brussels Sprouts

1/Microwave Brussels sprouts, green onion, celery and carrots until almost tender. Stir in tomatoes. Microwave until heated through.

2/Let stand, covered, while making yogurt sauce. Spoon hot sauce over vegetables before serving.

Zesty Brussels Sprouts

1 (10-oz.) pkg. frozen Brussels sprouts
1/4 cup chopped green onions
1/4 cup chopped celery
1/4 cup chopped carrots
2 tablespoons water
2 tablespoons butter or margarine
1 cup cherry tomatoes
1/2 cup plain yogurt
1 tablespoon all-purpose flour
2 teaspoons Dijon-style mustard
1 teaspoon prepared horseradish

1. In a deep 1-1/2-quart casserole with lid, combine Brussels sprouts, green onions, celery, carrots and water. Cover. Microwave at 100% (HIGH) 8 minutes or until almost tender; stir once. Drain well.
2. Stir in butter or margarine. Add cherry tomatoes. Cover. Microwave at 100% (HIGH) 2 to 3 minutes or until heated through. Let stand, covered, while making sauce.
3. In a small bowl, combine yogurt, flour, mustard and horseradish; whisk to mix well. Microwave at 30% (MEDIUM LOW) 3 minutes or until hot and thickened; stir every minute. Stir sauce; spoon over vegetables. Makes 3 to 4 servings.

Brussels Sprouts

1 lb. fresh Brussels sprouts
1/4 cup water

1. Trim off wilted outer leaves and excess stem from Brussels sprouts. Wash sprouts. Cut an X in bottom of each sprout. Halve any large sprouts.
2. In a 1-quart casserole with lid, combine sprouts and water. Cover. Microwave at 100% (HIGH) 8 to 9 minutes or until tender; stir once. Let stand, covered, 2 minutes. Drain. Makes 4 servings.

Maple Baked Beans

1 lb. dried pea beans (2 cups)
2 qts. water
1/4 teaspoon baking soda
6 cups water
1 teaspoon salt
8 bacon slices, crisp-cooked, crumbled
1/2 cup firmly packed brown sugar
1/2 cup maple-flavored syrup
2 teaspoons instant minced onion
2 teaspoons Worcestershire sauce
1 teaspoon ground cinnamon
2 apples, cored, sliced

---

1. Sort and rinse beans. In a deep 4-quart casserole with lid, combine beans and 2 quarts water. Stir in baking soda. Cover and let stand overnight.
2. Drain and rinse beans. Return beans to casserole. Add 6 cups water and salt. Cover and microwave at 100% (HIGH) 18 to 20 minutes or until boiling. Stir. Cover and microwave at 30% (MEDIUM LOW) 60 to 70 minutes or until beans are tender; stir every 20 minutes. Drain, reserving liquid.
3. Stir bacon, brown sugar, maple-flavored syrup, onion, Worcestershire sauce and cinnamon into beans. Add 1 cup reserved cooking liquid; reserve remaining liquid. Cover. Microwave at 30% (MEDIUM LOW) 80 to 90 minutes or until beans are very tender and flavors blend; stir every 20 minutes. Add more reserved cooking liquid, if necessary. Top with a ring of apple slices. Cover. Microwave at 30% (MEDIUM LOW) 15 to 20 minutes or until apples are tender; give dish a half turn after 10 minutes. Makes 6 to 8 servings.

Green Beans Italiano

1 (9-oz.) pkg. frozen Italian green beans
2 tablespoons water
1/2 (16-oz.) can garbanzo beans, drained
2 tablespoons chopped pimento
2 tablespoons sliced ripe olives
2 tablespoons chopped pepperoni
2 tablespoons olive oil
1/2 teaspoon dried leaf oregano, crushed
1/8 teaspoon garlic powder

To garnish:
Parsley sprigs
Pepperoni slices

---

1. In a deep 1-1/2-quart casserole with lid, combine Italian beans and water. Cover. Microwave at 100% (HIGH) 7 minutes or until tender; stir once. Drain well.
2. Add garbanzo beans, pimento, olives, pepperoni, olive oil, oregano and garlic powder; mix well. Cover. Microwave at 100% (HIGH) 2 minutes or until heated through; stir once. Garnish with parsley and pepperoni. Makes 3 to 4 servings.

Glazed Beets

2 (16-oz.) cans whole tiny beets, drained
2 tablespoons firmly packed brown sugar
2 teaspoons cornstarch
2/3 cup cranberry-juice cocktail
2 tablespoons white vinegar
1 teaspoon prepared horseradish
1/4 cup cranberry-orange relish

---

1. Place beets in a 2-quart casserole with lid; set aside. In a 2-cup glass measuring cup, mix brown sugar and cornstarch until well combined. Stir in cranberry-juice cocktail, vinegar and horseradish.
2. Microwave at 100% (HIGH) 2 to 2-1/2 minutes or until mixture thickens and bubbles; stir every minute. Stir in cranberry-orange relish. Gently mix sauce into beets. Cover. Microwave at 100% (HIGH) 7 minutes or until heated through. Makes 6 servings.

Green Beans Italiano

Carrot Coins

1 lb. carrots
1/4 cup water

1. Halve thick portion of carrots lengthwise. Slice 1/2 inch thick. In a 1-quart casserole with lid, combine carrot slices and water. Cover.
2. Microwave at 100% (HIGH) 11 to 12 minutes or until tender; stir after 5 minutes. Let stand, covered, 2 minutes. Drain. Makes 4 servings.

Fresh Cauliflowerets

1 (1-1/2-lb.) head cauliflower
1/4 cup water

1. Cut cauliflower into flowerets. Place in a 1-1/2-quart casserole with lid, with stems toward outside of dish. Add water; cover.
2. Microwave at 100% (HIGH) 7 to 8 minutes or until tender; stir after 4 minutes. Let stand, covered, 2 minutes. Drain. Makes 5 to 6 servings.

Crisp Fried Eggplant

1/2 medium eggplant (8 oz.)
1/2 cup all-purpose flour
1/2 cup milk
1 egg white
1/4 teaspoon onion salt
Seasoned dry bread crumbs
9 tablespoons vegetable oil

1. Cut eggplant crosswise into 12 to 14 thin slices, about 1/8 inch thick. Set aside.
2. Preheat a 10-inch microwave browning skillet at 100% (HIGH) 4 minutes.
3. In a pie plate, beat together flour, milk, egg white and onion salt. Place bread crumbs in a pie plate. Dip eggplant slices in batter, then in bread crumbs; press crumbs in with fingers. Place crumb-coated slices on a wire rack over waxed paper.
4. Add 3 tablespoons oil to preheated browning skillet. Quickly add 4 to 5 eggplant slices in a single layer. Microwave, uncovered, at 100% (HIGH) 1 minute. Turn slices; microwave at 100% (HIGH) 30 seconds or until tender.
5. Keep warm in a 200F (95C) oven while preparing remaining slices. Wipe out browning skillet with paper towels, being careful not to touch hot skillet.
6. Preheat browning skillet at 100% (HIGH) 3 minutes. Add 3 tablespoons oil. Quickly add 4 to 5 more crumb-coated slices; microwave as before. Repeat with remaining slices and oil, wiping out and preheating browning skillet as before. Makes 6 servings.

Fresh Mushroom Slices

2 tablespoons butter or margarine
2 cups sliced fresh mushrooms

1. Place butter or margarine in a 1-quart casserole with lid. Microwave at 100% (HIGH) 45 seconds or until melted.
2. Add mushrooms. Toss to coat. Cover. Microwave at 100% (HIGH) 3 to 4 minutes or until tender; stir after 2 minutes. Makes 2 servings.

How to Make Peas à la Française

1/Line a deep casserole with large lettuce leaves. In lettuce-lined casserole, gently combine frozen peas and onions, shredded lettuce, butter and sugar. The leaves provide moisture for cooking peas.

2/Serve peas with dollops of sour cream for a delightful sweet and sour flavor. Sprinkle chives over sour cream.

Peas à la Française

Several large iceberg-lettuce leaves
2 (10-oz.) pkgs. frozen peas and onions
2 cups shredded iceberg lettuce
2 tablespoons sugar
1/4 cup butter or margarine

To garnish:
Dairy sour cream
Chopped chives

1. Line a deep 2-quart casserole with a lid with large lettuce leaves. Break apart peas and onions with a fork. In lettuce-lined casserole, gently combine peas and onions, shredded lettuce, sugar and butter or margarine. Cover.
2. Microwave at 100% (HIGH) 10 minutes or until peas are tender, tossing gently after 5 minutes. Let stand, covered, 2 minutes. Serve topped with a dollop of sour cream and chives. Makes 6 servings.

Baked Potatoes

4 (6- to 8-oz.) baking potatoes

1. Pierce each potato several times with a large fork to allow steam to escape. Arrange potatoes, spoke-fashion, in a circle in microwave oven on a white paper towel.
2. Microwave at 100% (HIGH) 10 to 12 minutes or until potatoes are slightly firm when gently squeezed. Turn potatoes over and rearrange once after 5 minutes. Wrap in foil; let stand 5 minutes. Makes 4 servings.

How to Make Confetti-Stuffed Peppers

1/For precooking, pepper halves are placed cut-side down against baking dish to capture steam and speed cooking. Turn peppers cut-side up; drain before filling with creamed vegetable mixture.

2/Cook peppers until they are crisp-tender and filling is heated through. Slip a knife into center of filling to check if it is hot. Sprinkle with cracker crumbs after cooking; this prevents crumbs from getting soggy.

Taco Salad

6 cups torn mixed salad greens
1 (15-oz.) can red beans, drained, rinsed
1 avocado, sliced, dipped in lemon juice
2 tomatoes, cut in wedges
1/2 cup ripe olives, sliced
1 lb. ground beef
1/4 cup chopped green onions
2 to 4 tablespoons canned diced green chilies
1 cup taco sauce

To garnish:
1 cup shredded Cheddar cheese (4 oz.)
Corn chips

1. In a 4-quart salad bowl, arrange greens, beans, avocado, tomatoes and olives. Cover and refrigerate until serving time.
2. At serving time, crumble ground beef into a deep 1-1/2-quart casserole. Stir in green onions. Microwave at 100% (HIGH) 4 to 5 minutes or until meat is no longer pink and onion is tender; stir after 2 minutes. Drain.
3. Stir in chilies and taco sauce. Microwave at 100% (HIGH) 3 to 4 minutes or until boiling.
4. Pour over salad. Toss until combined. Garnish with cheese and corn chips. Serve immediately. Makes 6 servings.

Confetti-Stuffed Peppers

1 tablespoon butter or margarine
1/4 cup cheese-cracker crumbs
1 (8-oz.) pkg. frozen mixed vegetables with onion sauce
1/2 cup milk
1 tablespoon butter or margarine
1/4 cup instant-cooking rice
2 tablespoons chopped pimento
1/4 teaspoon dried leaf thyme, crushed
2 medium, green bell peppers, halved lengthwise

1. Place 1 tablespoon butter or margarine in a small bowl. Microwave at 100% (HIGH) 30 seconds or until melted. Stir in cracker crumbs; set aside.
2. In a 1-1/2-quart casserole with lid, combine frozen vegetables, milk and 1 tablespoon butter or margarine. Cover and microwave at 100% (HIGH) 6 minutes. Stir sauce after 3 minutes until smooth. When vegetables are tender, quickly stir in rice, pimento and thyme. Let stand, covered, 5 minutes.
3. Arrange peppers, cut-side down, in an 8-inch-square baking dish. Cover with vented plastic wrap. Microwave at 100% (HIGH) 5 minutes. Turn peppers cut-side up; drain off juices. Spoon creamed vegetables into peppers. Cover dish with vented plastic wrap. Microwave at 100% (HIGH) 4 minutes or until peppers are crisp-tender and filling is heated through. Slip a knife into center of filling to check that it is hot. Sprinkle with buttered cracker crumbs. Makes 4 servings.

Piña Colada Salad Mold

1 (8-oz.) can pineapple chunks, juice pack
1 (3-oz.) pkg. lemon-flavored gelatin
1/2 cup non-alcoholic Piña Colada drink mix
1/4 cup rum
2 tablespoons lemon juice
1/4 cup shredded coconut
1/4 cup chopped macadamia nuts
To garnish:
Lettuce leaves
Lime slices

1. Lightly oil a 3-cup mold. Drain pineapple, reserving juice. Add water to juice to make 1 cup. In a 1-1/2-quart bowl, microwave juice mixture at 100% (HIGH) 2-1/2 minutes or until boiling.
2. Stir in gelatin until completely dissolved. Stir in Piña Colada mix, rum and lemon juice. Refrigerate until almost set.
3. Fold in pineapple, coconut and nuts. Pour into oiled mold. Refrigerate until firm. Unmold on lettuce leaves; garnish with lime slices. Makes 4 servings.

Fresh Spinach

1 lb. fresh spinach (12 cups)

1. Wash and drain spinach. Trim off tough stem ends. Place spinach with water that clings to leaves in a deep 5-quart casserole with lid. Cover.
2. Microwave at 100% (HIGH) 9 to 10 minutes or until tender; stir after 4 minutes. Makes 4 servings.

Baked Sweet Potatoes or Yams

4 (6- to 8-oz.) sweet potatoes or yams

1. Pierce each potato several times with a large fork to allow steam to escape. Arrange potatoes, spoke-fashion, in a circle in microwave oven on white paper towels.
2. Microwave at 100% (HIGH) 11 to 14 minutes or until potatoes are slightly firm when gently squeezed. Turn potatoes over and rearrange after 5 minutes. Wrap in foil. Let stand 5 minutes. Makes 4 servings.

Spaghetti Squash Straw & Hay

1/4 cup butter or margarine
6 cups hot cooked spaghetti squash with shell, below
3/4 cup sliced cooked ham strips
1/2 cup cooked green peas
1 (2-1/2-oz.) jar sliced mushrooms, drained
2 egg yolks, beaten
1/2 pint whipping cream (1 cup)
1 cup grated Parmesan cheese (3 oz.)

1. In a large bowl, stir butter or margarine into hot squash until melted. Fold in ham, peas and mushrooms. In a small bowl, whisk egg yolks and cream until foamy. Slowly add cream mixture to squash mixture; mix well. Stir in 1/2 of Parmesan cheese.
2. Drain juices from baking dish used to cook squash. Mound squash mixture into 1 of the squash shells in a 13" x 9" baking dish. Cover with vented plastic wrap.
3. Microwave at 100% (HIGH) 7 to 10 minutes or until heated through and sauce has thickened; toss every 3 minutes. Top with remaining Parmesan cheese. Makes 6 servings.

Spaghetti Squash

1 (4-1/4-lb.) spaghetti squash
1/3 cup water

1. Place whole squash in a 13" x 9" baking dish. Microwave at 100% (HIGH) 10 minutes. Halve squash lengthwise. Remove seeds and membrane. Place squash, cut-side up, in same baking dish. Add water. Cover with vented plastic wrap.
2. Microwave at 100% (HIGH) 12 minutes; give dish a half turn after 6 minutes. Let stand, covered, 2 minutes. Squash should feel tender when pierced with a large fork and strands of squash should start to pull away from the shell. Makes 6 servings.

Succotash Scallop

1 (10-oz.) pkg. frozen baby lima beans
1 cup water
1 tablespoon butter or margarine
1/4 cup seasoned dry bread crumbs
2 tablespoons butter or margarine
2 tablespoons chopped onion
2 tablespoons chopped green bell pepper
2 teaspoons all-purpose flour
1/2 cup milk
1 cup shredded Monterey Jack cheese (4 oz.)
1 (8-3/4-oz.) can whole-kernel corn, drained
1/2 (8-oz.) can water chestnuts, drained, sliced
2 tablespoons chopped pimento
1/2 teaspoon celery seed

1. Combine lima beans and water in a deep 1-1/2-quart casserole with lid. Cover and microwave at 100% (HIGH) 11 minutes or until tender, stirring once. Drain. Place in a small bowl. Cover. Set aside.
2. In a small bowl, microwave 1 tablespoon butter or margarine at 100% (HIGH) 30 seconds or until melted. Stir in bread crumbs; set aside.
3. In same casserole, microwave 2 tablespoons butter or margarine, onion and green pepper at 100% (HIGH) 2-1/2 to 3 minutes or until vegetables are tender; stir after 1 minute. Stir in flour until blended; microwave at 100% (HIGH) 1 minute or until mixture bubbles. Gradually add milk.
4. Microwave at 100% (HIGH) 1-1/2 to 2 minutes or until thickened and bubbly; stir after 1 minute. Gradually add cheese; stir until melted. Stir in limas, corn, water chestnuts, pimento and celery seed. Cover. Microwave at 100% (HIGH) 6 minutes or until heated through. Top with buttered crumbs. Makes 4 servings.

Hot Slaw Mexicana

1/8 medium head cabbage
1/2 medium carrot
1/4 medium green bell pepper
1/2 cup cherry tomatoes
1/4 cup pitted ripe olives
1/4 cup whole-kernel corn, cooked, drained
1/2 cup shredded process pepper cheese or sharp process cheese (2 oz.)
1 tablespoon milk
1/2 teaspoon celery seed
1/8 teaspoon dry mustard
1/2 avocado, sliced

1. Using thin slicing blade on a food processor, slice cabbage, carrot, green pepper, cherry tomatoes and olives. Or slice finely by hand. Toss with corn in a deep 2-quart bowl; set aside.
2. In a medium bowl, combine cheese, milk, celery seed and dry mustard. Microwave at 30% (MEDIUM LOW) 2 to 2-1/2 minutes or until cheese has melted; stir every minute. Stir until smooth. Pour cheese dressing over cabbage mixture. Toss gently.
3. Cover with vented plastic wrap. Microwave at 100% (HIGH) 2 to 3 minutes or until heated through; stir once. Garnish with avocado slices. Serve salad hot. Makes 3 to 4 servings.

French Tossed Salad Mold

1 (1/4-oz.) envelope unflavored gelatin (1 tablespoon)
1-1/2 cups water
1/2 cup sweet red French dressing
1/2 cup finely chopped lettuce
2 tablespoons shredded carrot
2 tablespoons chopped green bell pepper
2 tablespoons chopped celery
2 tablespoons sliced ripe olives
2 tablespoons chopped green onion

To garnish:
Cherry tomatoes
Ripe olives
Celery leaves

1. Lightly oil a 2-1/2 cup ring mold. In a 1-quart bowl, combine gelatin and water. Let stand 3 minutes. Microwave at 100% (HIGH) 1-1/2 to 2 minutes or until gelatin dissolves. Stir in French dressing. Refrigerate until almost set.
2. Fold in lettuce, carrot, green pepper, celery, olives and green onion. Turn into oiled mold. Refrigerate until set.
3. Unmold on a platter. Garnish with cherry tomatoes, olives and celery leaves. Makes 4 servings.

Bread & Cereal Products

Q. What are the advantages of defrosting and cooking breads and grains in the microwave?

A. Convenience breads defrost and heat in a matter of minutes. Keep a variety of breads and rolls on hand for sandwiches. Use the microwave to defrost only the number of slices or rolls needed. You can cook and eat hot cereals right in the heat-proof serving bowls.

Q. What are the disadvantages of cooking breads and grains in the microwave?

A. Compared with conventionally baked bread, yeast breads baked in the microwave are pale, low in volume and tough. Quick breads end up pale and raise and cook unevenly. Microwaved breads do not brown, but this can be partially overcome by using toppings, frostings and dark flours. It is easy to overcook breads in the microwave. This results in a dry, tough and hard product. Although rice and pasta do not cook any faster in the microwave, they can be cooked successfully.

Q. Which breads or grains do not cook satisfactorily in the microwave?

A. Yeast breads, homemade pizza with yeast crust, refrigerated rolls, baking-powder biscuits and quick-bread loaves are much better when baked conventionally.

Q. How do you know when breads and grains are done?

A. As in conventional baking, a wooden pick inserted in the center of a quick bread, muffin or coffeecake should come out clean. Hot cereal, rice and pasta should be cooked until tender.

Q. How do you reheat breads and grains in the microwave?

A. Reheat breads on a white paper towel so the bottom won't get soggy. You can reheat breads and rolls in a straw basket if the basket has no metal parts. Anything sugary, such as raisins, jelly filling or frosting, will become hot very quickly. Baked breads, rolls and sandwiches should be heated only until warm. If they are heated beyond this point in the microwave, they will become tough and hard.

Q. Are any special utensils needed for cooking breads and grains in the microwave?

A. It's handy to have a plastic or ceramic microwave muffin dish, but several glass or ceramic baking cups will do. Large microwave baking sheets or pizza plates are useful for heating several sandwiches at once.

Quick Breads in the Microwave

Quick breads that contain molasses, brown sugar, whole-wheat flour, chocolate or spices have a more attractive color than those made from plain batters. Topping quick breads with crumbs, streusel or sugar and cinnamon before baking will hide the fact that they are not browned.

Swiss Club Sandwich, page 68

ABC Sandwiches

1/4 cup chopped blanched almonds
4 bacon slices, crisp-cooked, crumbled
3/4 cup shredded sharp Cheddar cheese (3 oz.)
1/4 cup mayonnaise
1-1/2 teaspoons prepared horseradish
Pepper
4 French-bread slices

1. Place almonds in a 9-inch pie plate. Microwave at 100% (HIGH) 1-1/2 minutes or until lightly toasted.
2. In a medium bowl, combine bacon, cheese, mayonnaise, horseradish and toasted almonds. Season with pepper.
3. Spread almond mixture on bread slices. Line a 12-inch-round microwave platter with white paper towels. Place sandwiches on towel-lined microwave platter. Microwave at 100% (HIGH) 1-1/2 minutes or until cheese melts; give dish a half turn after 30 seconds. Serve immediately. Makes 4 sandwiches.

Quick-Cooking Rolled Oats

3 cups hot water
1-1/2 cups quick-cooking rolled oats
1/2 teaspoon salt

To serve:
Milk or half and half
Brown sugar
Cinnamon or nutmeg

1. Place hot water into a deep 2-quart casserole. Stir in cereal and salt.
2. Microwave at 100% (HIGH) 4-1/2 minutes or until water is nearly all absorbed. Stir well every 2 minutes. Stir before serving. Serve with milk or half and half, brown sugar and cinnamon or nutmeg. Makes 4 servings.

Strawberry-Jam Kuchen

Streusel Topping:
1/2 cup all-purpose flour
1/4 cup granulated sugar
1/4 cup firmly packed brown sugar
2 teaspoons ground cinnamon
3 tablespoons butter or margarine
1 egg yolk

Kuchen:
2 cups packaged biscuit mix
2 tablespoons sugar
1 egg
2/3 cup milk
1/2 cup strawberry jam

To serve:
Powdered sugar
Strawberries, if desired

1. To prepare topping, in a medium bowl, mix flour, granulated sugar, brown sugar and cinnamon. With a pastry blender or 2 knives, cut in butter or margarine and egg yolk until crumbly. Set aside.
2. Grease bottom of a round 8-inch baking dish. To make kuchen, in a medium bowl, combine biscuit mix, sugar, egg and milk; mix well. Beat vigorously by hand 30 seconds. Spread batter in greased baking dish.
3. Spoon jam in dollops over batter. Swirl through with a knife to marble. Sprinkle topping over batter. Microwave, uncovered, at 30% (MEDIUM LOW) 7 minutes; give dish a half turn after 4 minutes. Microwave at 100% (HIGH) 3 minutes or until a wooden pick inserted in center of cake comes out clean; give dish a half turn after 1-1/2 minutes.
4. Cool cake on a flat heatproof surface 15 minutes. Cut cake in wedges while warm. To serve, sprinkle with powdered sugar; garnish with strawberries, if desired. Makes 6 to 8 servings.

How to Make Strawberry-Jam Kuchen

1/Spread batter in a round 8-inch baking dish. Spoon strawberry jam over top of batter. Then, with a knife, swirl through batter to marble jam.

2/For Streusel Topping, use a pastry blender or 2 knives to cut butter or margarine into flour, sugar and cinnamon. Topping should resemble fine crumbs.

3/Sprinkle Streusel Topping evenly over top of batter.

4/Garnish cake with fresh strawberries and powdered sugar. Cut in wedges; serve with hot coffee or tea.

Parmesan-Spaghetti Ring

1/4 cup butter or margarine
10 oz. spaghetti, cooked, drained
2/3 cup grated Parmesan cheese
3 eggs, beaten
1 (3-1/2-oz.) can chopped mushrooms, drained
2 tablespoons chopped parsley
1 (16-oz.) jar spaghetti sauce

1. Oil a 5-cup microwave ring mold. In a large bowl, add butter or margarine to hot cooked spaghetti. Using 2 forks, gently lift spaghetti until butter or margarine is melted. Stir in Parmesan cheese; then stir in eggs. Stir in mushrooms and parsley.
2. Turn into oiled mold. Cover with vented plastic wrap. Microwave at 100% (HIGH) 5 minutes or until set. Cover with foil to keep warm.
3. Pour spaghetti sauce into a 1-quart casserole with lid. Cover. Microwave at 100% (HIGH) 5 minutes or until heated through; stir after 2-1/2 minutes. Slide knife around edge of mold to loosen spaghetti ring. Turn ring out onto a serving plate. Serve with spaghetti sauce. Makes 6 servings.

Crab Sandwiches Supreme

1 (7-1/2-oz.) can Alaskan king crab, drained, flaked
1/4 cup diced celery
1/2 (4-oz.) carton semi-soft natural cheese with garlic
  and herbs
2 tablespoons minced green onion
2 tablespoons grated Parmesan cheese
2 tablespoons lemon juice
2 tablespoons capers, drained
2 tablespoons mayonnaise
Dash pepper
6 hamburger buns, split

1. In a medium bowl, combine crab, celery, semi-soft cheese, green onion, Parmesan cheese, lemon juice, capers, mayonnaise and pepper. Mix well. Spread 1/4 cup of mixture on each of 4 hamburger buns using about 1/4 cup mixture for each.
2. Replace tops of buns; wrap each in a paper towel. Place wrapped buns on a microwave platter or tray in a circle. Microwave at 100% (HIGH) 2-1/2 minutes or until heated through; give plate a half turn after 1-1/2 minutes. Makes 6 servings.

Swiss Club Sandwiches

1 cup diced cooked chicken
1/4 cup chopped celery
1/4 cup sliced pimento-stuffed green olives
1 tablespoon chopped green onion
2 tablespoons crumbled blue cheese
1/4 cup mayonnaise or salad dressing
8 slices plain zwieback, 3-1/2 x 1-1/2 inches or
  4 plain rusks, 3-1/2 inches in diameter
4 tomato slices
12 cooked asparagus spears, well-drained
2 Swiss-cheese slices, halved crosswise
6 crisp-cooked bacon slices

1. In a medium bowl, combine chicken, celery, olives, green onion, blue cheese and mayonnaise or salad dressing. Mix gently.
2. Arrange 2 zwieback or 1 rusk for each serving in a 12" x 7" baking dish. Spoon chicken mixture onto zwieback or rusks. Top each with tomato slices, asparagus spears and Swiss-cheese slices. Crumble bacon over each serving. Microwave at 100% (HIGH) 3-1/2 to 4 minutes or until heated through. Makes 4 servings.

Herbed French Loaf

1 (8-oz.) French-bread loaf
1/2 cup butter or margarine
2 teaspoons dried leaf oregano
2 teaspoons dried leaf basil
1 teaspoon celery seeds
1/2 teaspoon onion powder
1/2 teaspoon sesame seeds

1. Cut French bread in 1-inch slices, cutting to, but not quite through, bottom of loaf.
2. In a small bowl, microwave butter or margarine at 10% (LOW) 1-1/2 to 2 minutes or until softened. Stir in oregano, basil, celery seeds and onion powder. Spread between bread slices and over top of loaf. Sprinkle with sesame seeds.
3. Line a platter with paper towels. Place loaf on paper-towel-lined platter. Microwave at 100% (HIGH) 1 to 1-1/2 minutes or until warm. Makes 4 to 6 servings.

Taco Hot Dogs

2 tablespoons taco sauce
1/2 cup shredded Cheddar cheese (2 oz.)
2 tablespoons chopped onion
2 tablespoons chopped canned green chilies
4 hot dogs
4 taco shells

To serve:
Shredded lettuce
Canned marinated garbanzo beans, drained
Frozen guacamole dip, thawed

1. In medium bowl, combine taco sauce, cheese, onion and chilies. Slit hot dogs lengthwise, but not quite through. Stuff with 3/4 of cheese mixture. Place in taco shells. Stand stuffed taco shells upright in a 12" x 7" baking dish. If needed, support shells with crumpled waxed paper.
2. Spoon remaining cheese mixture over top. Microwave at 100% (HIGH) 1-1/2 to 2 minutes or until heated through. To serve, top with shredded lettuce, garbanzo beans and guacamole dip. Makes 4 servings.

Variation
Beef Tacos: For 4 servings, crumble 1/2 pound ground beef into a 1-quart casserole. Cover loosely with waxed paper. Microwave at 100% (HIGH) 4 minutes or until meat is no longer pink; stir after 2 minutes. Drain well. Stir in 1/4 cup taco sauce, 1/2 cup shredded Cheddar cheese, 2 tablespoons chopped onion and 2 tablespoons chopped green chilies. Spoon into 4 taco shells. Microwave and serve as above.

How to Make Spanish Rice

1/Add chopped tomatoes, tomato-juice mixture and celery salt to cooked onions and pepper; microwave until boiling. Add rice. Stir until moistened. Cover and microwave until tender.

2/Sprinkle bacon and shredded cheese in a ring around casserole edge. Garnish center with green-pepper rings. Microwave a short time to melt cheese.

Spanish Rice

6 bacon slices
1/2 cup chopped onion
1/2 cup chopped green bell pepper
1 (28-oz.) can tomatoes
1/2 teaspoon celery salt
3/4 cup long-grain rice
1/2 cup shredded process American cheese (2 oz.)

To garnish:
Green-bell-pepper rings

1. Place bacon on a microwave rack in a 12" x 7" baking dish. Cover with a white paper towel. Microwave at 100% (HIGH) 4 to 5 minutes or until crisp. Measure about 1/4 cup bacon drippings into a deep 2-quart casserole with lid. Crumble bacon; set aside.
2. Add onion and green pepper to drippings in casserole. Microwave at 100% (HIGH) 5 minutes or until tender; stir after 3 minutes. Drain tomato juice into a 2-cup measuring cup; add enough water to make 1-1/2 cups. Chop tomatoes. Stir in tomatoes, tomato-juice mixture and celery salt. Cover. Microwave at 100% (HIGH) 6 to 8 minutes or until boiling.
3. Add rice. Stir until moistened. Cover. Microwave at 30% (MEDIUM LOW) 25 to 30 minutes or until rice is tender; stir every 10 minutes. Sprinkle bacon and cheese over mixture. Garnish with green-pepper rings. Microwave, uncovered, at 100% (HIGH) 1 minute or until cheese is melted. Makes 4 to 6 servings.

Microwaved Rice

2-1/4 cups hot water
1 tablespoon butter or margarine
1/4 teaspoon salt
1 cup long-grain rice

1. In a deep 2-quart casserole with lid, combine hot water, butter or margarine and salt. Cover. Microwave at 100% (HIGH) 4 to 5 minutes or until boiling. Stir in rice; cover.
2. Microwave at 30% (MEDIUM LOW) 20 minutes or until tender; stir after 10 minutes. Let stand, covered, 5 minutes. Fluff with a fork. Makes 4 to 5 (1-cup) servings.

Desserts

Q. Which kinds of desserts are most suitable for the microwave?

A. Puddings cooked this way are extra smooth and creamy. All fruit-based desserts have an excellent fresh flavor because of the fast cooking.

Q. Which desserts do not cook satisfactorily in the microwave?

A. Drop cookies cook so unevenly that they are not recommended. Some are burned while others are still doughy. The pastry in a two-crust pie does not cook but the filling heats rapidly. The solution is to make deep-dish pies, or microwave the pastry shell first. The top crust is microwaved separately; then the pie is assembled before serving. Custard in a large pie plate and dessert soufflés overcook on the edges before the center sets. It is difficult to obtain consistently good results with cakes made from scratch. Microwave baking results are more predictable with pudding-type cake mixes. Cream puffs, angel-food cakes, chiffon cakes and meringues should not be attempted because they need the heat from a conventional oven to rise.

Q. Can cakes and pastries be cooked in the microwave?

A. Yes. Cakes do not brown in the microwave but they do have an excellent light, airy texture. Because cakes are usually frosted, glazed or dusted with powdered sugar, the lack of browning is easily disguised. Pastry does not brown in the microwave. But microwave cooking makes the flakiest pastry you have ever tasted.

Q. How do you know when desserts are done?

A. A wooden pick inserted in the center of a cake should come out clean. Pudding should be thick and smooth. Each recipe has a doneness test to guide you.

Q. Are any special utensils needed to microwave desserts?

A. You must have a special microwave fluted tube pan in order to make tube cakes. Pans are available both in ceramic and plastic. Some care has to be taken when you select a pie plate. You will find that not all 9-inch pie plates will hold the same amount. Measure how much water your pie plate will hold, then measure how much pie filling you have. Choose a glass or ceramic pie plate that is large enough for the pie filling required in the recipe.

Pie plates—Both pie plates are marked as 10-inch plates but one holds 7 cups and the other holds 4-1/2 cups!

Devonshire Cheesecake Cups, page 75

Peach-Parfait Pie

1 (3-oz.) pkg. lemon-flavored gelatin
1-1/4 cups water
1 pint peach ice cream
1 cup thawed frozen whipped topping
1 Pastry Shell, or Crumb Crust, page 74

To garnish:
Whipped topping
Peach slices
Mint sprig

---

1. In a 2-quart bowl, combine gelatin and water. Microwave at 100% (HIGH) 2 to 3 minutes or until gelatin dissolves; stir every minute. Add several scoops of ice cream to hot gelatin. Stir until ice cream is melted. Stir in remaining ice cream.
2. Stir whipped topping; stir into ice-cream mixture. Whisk until smooth. Refrigerate 40 to 45 minutes or until mixture mounds when dropped from a spoon.
3. Spoon into pastry shell or crumb crust. Refrigerate 8 hours or overnight or until firm. Garnish with whipped topping, peach slices and a mint sprig. Makes 6 servings.

Variations
Raspberry-Parfait Pie: Substitute raspberry-flavored gelatin for lemon gelatin and frozen raspberry yogurt or sherbet for peach ice cream. Garnish with fresh or frozen raspberries.
Lime-Parfait Pie: Substitute lime-flavored gelatin for lemon gelatin and lime sherbet for peach ice cream. Garnish with fresh lime slices.

Toasted-Almond Cake Roll

2 cups slivered blanched almonds (7-1/2 oz.)
3/4 teaspoon baking powder
4 egg whites
4 egg yolks
1/2 cup powdered sugar
1 teaspoon vanilla extract
1/4 teaspoon almond extract
Powdered sugar

Cocoa-Fluff Filling:
1 envelope dessert-topping mix
1/2 cup cold milk
1/2 teaspoon vanilla extract
1/4 cup chocolate-drink mix

---

1. Spread almonds in a 12-inch-square microwave baker. Microwave at 100% (HIGH) 4 to 5 minutes or until toasted; stir every 1-1/2 minutes. Cool to room temperature. Grind almonds or process until fine in a food processor fitted with the steel blade in 2 or 3 batches. Measure 1-1/2 cups. Stir baking powder into ground almonds; set aside.
2. Line same microwave baker with waxed paper cut long enough to extend over ends of baking dish. Butter top of waxed paper where it touches bottom of dish.
3. In a large bowl, beat egg whites with an electric mixer on high speed until stiff but not dry. In a large bowl, combine egg yolks, 1/2 cup powdered sugar, vanilla and almond extract. With an electric mixer on high speed, beat mixture 3 to 5 minutes or until thick and lemon-colored. Stir nut mixture into yolk mixture. Fold in beaten egg whites. Spread batter evenly in prepared baking dish.
4. Microwave at 100% (HIGH) 6 minutes or until a wooden pick inserted in center of cake comes out clean. Let stand 1 minute. Using extended ends of waxed paper, lift cake out of dish. Place on a wire rack. Immediately cover with a damp cloth towel. Cool 50 to 60 minutes.
5. To prepare filling, in a deep bowl, combine dessert-topping mix, milk, vanilla and drink mix. Beat with an electric mixer on high speed until peaks form. Beat about 2 minutes or until smooth and fluffy.
6. To serve, remove towel. Spread filling on cooled cake. Roll up, jelly-roll style, peeling off waxed paper as cake is rolled. Be careful not to roll too tightly. Sprinkle top of roll with additional powdered sugar. Makes 6 to 8 servings.

How to Make Toasted-Almond Cake Roll

1/Microwave cake in a baking dish lined with waxed paper. Waxed paper is cut long enough so ends may be used to lift cake from baking dish to cooling rack.

2/Remove cake from baking dish; place it on a wire rack. Immediately cover cake completely with a damp towel 50 to 60 minutes. This keeps cake moist enough to roll.

3/Spread cooled cake with Cocoa-Fluff Filling. Carefully roll up cake, jelly-roll style, peeling off waxed paper as cake is rolled. Do not try to roll cake too tightly or it may crack.

4/Sprinkle roll lightly with powdered sugar. Use a serrated knife to slice cake roll. Lift slices with a serving spatula.

Gingerbread

1 (14.5-oz.) pkg. gingerbread mix

1. Place a 2-inch diameter jar in center of an 8-inch-round cake dish.

2. In a medium bowl, prepare gingerbread mix as directed on package. Pour batter into dish around jar. Microwave, uncovered, at 100% (HIGH) 8 to 9 minutes. Give dish a quarter turn every 2 minutes. When done, top of gingerbread is almost dry and springs back when lightly touched. A wooden pick inserted off-center will come out clean.

3. Cool 10 minutes in pan on a flat heatproof surface. Twist jar and remove. Cut into wedges; serve warm. Makes 6 to 8 servings.

Peanut-Brickle Layer Bars

1/4 cup butter or margarine
1 cup peanut-butter-cookie crumbs
1 cup peanut-butter-flavored baking pieces
1 (6-oz.) pkg. almond-brickle baking pieces
1 (3-1/2-oz.) can flaked coconut (1-1/3 cups)
1/2 cup salted peanuts, chopped
1 (14-oz.) can sweetened condensed milk (1-1/3 cups)

1. Place a 2-inch diameter jar in center of a 12" x 7" baking dish. Place butter or margarine in baking dish. Microwave at 100% (HIGH) 1 minute or until melted. Stir in cookie crumbs. Press into bottom of baking dish around jar.
2. Sprinkle with peanut-butter pieces, almond-brickle pieces, coconut and peanuts. Spoon condensed milk evenly over all. Microwave, uncovered, at 100% (HIGH) 7 to 8 minutes or until set in center when lightly touched; give dish a half turn after 4 minutes. Cool completely on a wire rack; twist out jar. Cut into bars. Makes 48 bars.

Pastry Shell

1-1/2 sticks pie-crust mix
3 tablespoons water

1. Prepare pie-crust mix with water according to package directions. On a lightly floured surface, roll out dough 1/8 inch thick. Cut circle of dough 2 inches larger than top of pie plate. Gently fit pastry in pie plate. Fold under edge and flute. Prick all over bottom and side of pastry with a fork.
2. Microwave at 70% (MEDIUM HIGH) 7 to 9 minutes or until done; give dish a half turn after 4 minutes. If dough puffs up during cooking, gently prick with a fork. Cool on a wire rack before filling. Makes 1 (9- or 10-inch) shell.

Bananas-Foster Chiffon Pie

1 (9-inch) Crumb Crust, below, made with vanilla wafers
1 (1/4-oz.) envelope unflavored gelatin (1 tablespoon)
2/3 cup firmly packed brown sugar
4 egg yolks
1/2 cup mashed ripe bananas
1/4 cup dark rum
1 teaspoon grated lemon peel
4 egg whites
1/4 teaspoon cream of tartar
2/3 cup firmly packed brown sugar
1 cup banana-flavored yogurt

To garnish:
Whipped cream
Sliced bananas dipped in lemon juice
Mint sprig

1. Prepare crust using vanilla wafers; set aside.
2. In a 1-1/2-quart bowl, thoroughly combine gelatin and 2/3 cup brown sugar; set aside.
3. In a medium bowl, with an electric mixer on medium speed, beat egg yolks, bananas, rum and lemon peel until blended. Stir into gelatin mixture. Microwave at 30% (MEDIUM LOW) 6 to 7 minutes or until mixture almost boils and gelatin is dissolved; stir every 1-1/2 minutes. Refrigerate until mixture mounds when dropped from a spoon.
4. In another medium bowl, with an electric mixer on high speed, beat egg whites and cream of tartar until soft peaks form. Gradually add 2/3 cup brown sugar; beat until stiff and glossy. Fold banana mixture into egg-white mixture. Fold in banana yogurt. Spoon into pie crust. Refrigerate 8 hours or overnight or until set.
5. Garnish with whipped cream, banana slices and mint. Makes 6 servings.

Crumb Crust

6 tablespoons butter or margarine
1-1/2 cups fine graham-cracker, vanilla-cookie or chocolate-wafer crumbs
3 tablespoons sugar

1. Lightly butter a 9-inch pie plate. Place butter or margarine in a 1-1/2-quart bowl. Microwave at 100% (HIGH) 45 to 60 seconds or until melted. Stir in crumbs and sugar until all crumbs are moistened. Spoon crumb mixture over bottom and side of pie plate. Press crumbs firmly and evenly over bottom and side of pie plate.
2. Microwave at 100% (HIGH) 1-1/2 to 2 minutes or until set; give dish a half turn after 1 minute. Quickly press crumbs firmly against pie plate again. Cool before filling. Makes 1 (9-inch) crust.

How to Make Bananas-Foster Chiffon Pie

1/Thoroughly combine unflavored gelatin and brown sugar. Mixing gelatin with sugar helps prevent lumping. Stir in egg-yolk mixture; microwave until mixture begins to boil.

2/Beat egg whites until soft peaks form. Beat in brown sugar.

3/Beat brown sugar into egg whites until stiff and glossy. At stiff-peak stage, a rubber spatula should leave a clean trough through egg whites.

4/Garnish with whipped cream, banana slices and mint. To loosen crumb crust, wrap a hot wet towel around pie plate for a few minutes before serving.

Devonshire Cheesecake Cups

6 vanilla wafers
1 (8-oz.) pkg. cream cheese
1/3 cup firmly packed brown sugar
1 egg
1/2 teaspoon vanilla extract

To garnish:
Dairy sour cream
Green grapes or strawberries
Brown sugar

1. Place paper baking cups in 6 (6-ounce) custard cups. Place a vanilla wafer in each paper baking cup; set aside.

2. Unwrap cream cheese; place in a 1-1/2-quart bowl. Microwave at 10% (LOW) 1-1/2 to 2 minutes or until softened. Add brown sugar, egg and vanilla. Beat with an electric mixer on high speed until smooth.
3. Pour into paper baking cups. Arrange in a circle in microwave. Microwave at 30% (MEDIUM LOW) 7 to 8 minutes; rearrange cups after 4 minutes. Remove any cheesecake cups that are set in center or those in which a knife inserted off-center comes out clean.
4. Microwave remaining cheesecake cups at 30% (MEDIUM LOW) 1 minute or until done. Cool on a wire rack 1 hour. Refrigerate. Serve topped with dollops of sour cream, green-grape clusters or strawberries and a sprinkling of brown sugar. Makes 6 servings.

Café au Lait Soufflé

2 teaspoons unflavored gelatin powder
2 tablespoons sugar
2 egg yolks
1/2 cup cold strong coffee
2 tablespoons coffee-flavored liqueur
2 egg whites
1/8 teaspoon cream of tartar
2 tablespoons sugar
1/2 cup whipping cream, whipped

To garnish:
Whipped cream, if desired
Chocolate curls, if desired

---

1. In a 1-quart bowl, thoroughly mix gelatin and 2 tablespoons sugar. In a medium bowl, with an electric mixer at low speed, beat egg yolks and coffee until blended. Stir into gelatin mixture. Microwave at 30% (MEDIUM LOW) 4 to 4-1/2 minutes or until mixture almost boils and gelatin is dissolved; stir every minute. Stir in liqueur. Refrigerate 1 to 1-1/2 hours or until mixture mounds when dropped from a spoon; stir frequently.
2. In another medium bowl, with an electric mixer at high speed, beat egg whites and cream of tartar until soft peaks form. Gradually add remaining 2 tablespoons sugar; beating until stiff and glossy. Fold coffee mixture into egg-white mixture. Fold in whipped cream. Spoon into a 1-quart soufflé dish or 3 to 4 (10-oz.) cups. Refrigerate 3 to 4 hours or until firm.
3. Garnish with whipped cream and chocolate curls, if desired. Makes 3 to 4 servings.

Luscious Strawberry Trifle

1 (4-1/2-oz.) pkg. golden egg-custard mix
3 cups milk
1/2 teaspoon orange-flavored extract
1/4 teaspoon grated orange peel
8 (1-oz.) sponge-cake dessert cups
1/4 cup orange-flavored liqueur
1/4 cup orange marmalade
4 cups sliced fresh strawberries
2 cups thawed frozen whipped topping

To decorate:
Whipped topping, if desired
Fresh whole strawberries

---

1. Empty custard mix into a bowl. Gradually stir in milk. Microwave, uncovered, at 100% (HIGH) 5 minutes. Stir well. Microwave at 100% (HIGH) 3 minutes or until mixture comes to a boil; stir once; sauce will be thin. Stir in orange extract and orange peel. Refrigerate only 15 minutes.
2. Arrange 4 sponge-cake dessert cups in a 2-1/2-quart glass serving bowl; cut cakes as necessary to fit dish. Prick cakes all over with a fork. Drizzle with 1/2 of orange-flavored liqueur.
3. Spread with 1/2 of orange marmalade. Top with 1/2 of strawberries. Pour 1/2 of custard sauce over strawberries, being sure part of custard flows through to cake layer. Repeat layers of cake, liqueur, marmalade, strawberries and custard sauce. Spread top with whipped topping. Refrigerate several hours.
4. Immediately before serving, decorate with additional whipped topping, if desired, and whole strawberries. Makes 8 to 10 servings.

Cake-Mix Layer Cake

1 cake mix with pudding in the mix

1. Prepare cake batter as directed on package. Line bottoms of 2 (8-inch) round cake dishes with waxed paper. Divide cake batter evenly between dishes.
2. Microwave 1 layer at a time, uncovered, at 30% (MEDIUM LOW) 6 minutes. Give dish a quarter turn. Microwave at 100% (HIGH) 3-1/2 to 5 minutes; give dish a quarter turn after 2 minutes. When done, top of cake is slightly moist and springs back when lightly touched in center. A wooden pick inserted in center of cake will come out clean.
3. Run a knife around edge of cake to loosen from dish. Immediately invert cake on a heatproof surface covered with waxed paper. Carefully peel waxed paper from layer bottom. Repeat with second layer. Cool before frosting. Makes 2 (8-inch) layers.

Creamy Butterscotch Frosting

**2 (6-oz.) pkgs. butterscotch-flavored pieces (about
  1-1/2 cups)**
1/2 cup butter or margarine
1/2 pint dairy sour cream (1 cup)
2 teaspoons vanilla extract
1 (1-lb.) box powdered sugar (about 5 cups)

1. In a 1-1/2-quart bowl, combine butterscotch pieces and butter or margarine. Microwave at 100% (HIGH) 2 minutes or until chips melt. Stir after 1 minute and again after 1-1/2 minutes.
2. Stir until smooth. Cool to room temperature.
3. Stir in sour cream and vanilla. With an electric mixer on medium speed, gradually beat in powdered sugar until mixture is a good consistency for spreading. Use frosting to fill and frost an 8-inch, 2-layer cake. Store frosted cake in refrigerator. Makes 4 cups of frosting or enough to frost a 2-layer cake.

Baked Apples

4 (6- to 7-oz.) baking apples
1/4 cup raisins
1/2 cup firmly packed brown sugar
Ground cinnamon
Ground nutmeg
1/4 cup bourbon or apple juice
Vanilla ice cream or whipping cream

1. Remove tops of cores but do not cut through bottoms. Peel a small strip around top of each apple. Set apples, stem-side up, in an 8-inch-square baking dish. Spoon raisins into center of each apple. Mound brown sugar on apples. Sprinkle with cinnamon and nutmeg. Drizzle with bourbon or apple juice.
2. Cover with vented plastic wrap. Microwave at 100% (HIGH) 7 to 9 minutes; give dish a half turn after 4 minutes. Let stand, covered, 10 minutes. Apple should be tender when pierced with a fork. If not, recover and microwave 1 to 2 minutes more. Spoon pan juices over apples. Serve with vanilla ice cream or cream. Makes 4 servings.

Cake-Mix Layer Cake with Creamy Butterscotch Frosting

Index